THE
NEW
CONSCIOUSNESS

Other books by
Obadiah Silas Harris;

Self Knowledge and Social Action

THE
NEW
CONSCIOUSNESS

OBADIAH SILAS HARRIS

Arizona State University

PENDELL
PUBLISHING
COMPANY

Library of Congress Catalog Card Number: 76-57918

International Standard Book Number: 0-87812-151-X

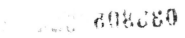

TABLE OF CONTENTS

PREFACE

Man is so accustomed to mental consciousness that he can hardly imagine a lesser consciousness in the past or a greater one in the future. He is now on a plateau from which he ordinarily looks neither to the trail below nor the peaks above. Yet mental consciousness was once unknown on earth. It was a bold adventurer and a stranger, incipient and rudimentary in the evolution, long before it developed into human reason. Even today the mental consciousness on earth exists in man but not in many lower forms of life.

Now a *new and higher consciousness* is preparing for those who can receive and take advantage of its presence. On this rests the hope of the future and the destiny of man. For all difficulties will be laid on it and overcome which the man of mental consciousness has proven unable to master.

This *new consciousness* is as certain to appear and predominate in the days ahead as reason was in the past and to become more powerful and profound than reason ever has been or can be. We must choose to grow and rise and unite in the light of this *new consciousness*. Otherwise, as human experience shows, it will be imposed upon us, perhaps through harsh catastrophe, by the evolution of nature and the divine call for the progress of the race.

CHAPTER I

IN THE BEGINNING

IN THE BEGINNING

(The Story of Creation)

Among the oldest and most persistent inquiries of man is that which calls for an explanation of creation sufficient to satisfy his soul and his intellect. We desire to have this story unfolded in full and our own part in it made as clear and meaningful as possible. Deep within ourselves we feel that we are more than a pawn of time and circumstance to whom, as in Shakespeare's play someone says, "Out, brief candle." There is a light in us which is not a brief candle but an eternal spark, and we would find the divine flame from which it was kindled in the beginning.

For the answer to this inquiry, man long ago turned first to religion, and much later to science. At first religion and science seemed at hopeless odds on this question. Men were told that they would have to choose the answer of religion or that of science, but not both. No middle ground or conciliation seemed possible.

Not only were people forced to choose, but sometimes they were punished or made to recant if they chose the standpoint of science. This situation has now gone full circle. Nowadays in Communist countries the government restricts or punishes those who subscribe to the religious explanation of creation and existence; but in the free religious countries of the world, including (I am glad to say) our own United States, these uncomprehending positions in the main have been abandoned.

It is true that in some parts of the country individuals will occasionally object to the teaching in the schools of the theories of science regarding creation and evolution. But on the whole, deeper insights and reasonable interpretations on both sides have resulted in a broader outlook in the free world, in which conciliation between them on this subject is made possible. For example, the Pope took no exception to the interpretation that the six Biblical days of Creation mentioned in Genesis could be understood to signify not 24-hour days, but periods of geologic time, each covering millions or billionsof years.

Religion antedated science by far in narrating the origin and history of creation. The accounts of the several religions on this score vary widely. They range from the Judeo-Christian detailed account of Genesis to the extreme opposite of the Buddhist view, which explains away creation by saying that it was never created, that the world and the people, creatures, and things in it are an illusion, and a non-reality.

Religion is not alone in this plurality of creation views. Science differs as widely or more so on this point. Science has many conflicting theories on creation, and no certainty about any of them. Neither religion nor science can point the finger at each other in this regard. Science has not come even remotely close to settling on a theory which it can today hold up as the sole explanation of creation. Some scientists say that it came about as the result of a vast explosion of an original gaseous material, but what the gas was, and who made it, or where it came from they cannot tell.

One of the greatest of modern scientists, Einstein, summed it up by saying that all science can offer is a number of theories, about none of which it is certain. But there was no doubt in Einstein's mind of the certitude of a Divine Author of creation. He said that when he looked at the stars and the universe, he felt awe and wonder before the creative power of God. Einstein saw no contradiction here. To him Science is man endeavoring to gain a better understanding of natural processes, while God is the Creator of nature and man, and infinitely greater and beyond both.

In fact, there is a close resemblance between the creation account of Genesis in the Bible, written thousands of years ago, and the findings of Science in the modern era through its branches that deal with this subject, such as geology, anthropology, botany, zoology, chemistry, physics, and others. In its broad outlines the creation according to Genesis, at least as to the physical aspects, would fit generally into scientific textbooks.

Genesis says of the creation that the earth was at first without form and void, which conforms to a gaseous condition. Next, it was covered with water and God moved on the surface of the water. Then light and darkness came, day and night. Next the dry land emerged from the water, after which the land became covered with plants and vegetation.

There followed living creatures and birds, fish and water creatures, cattle and beasts of the field, in that order, which lived upon the vegetation or upon each other. Finally, and last, came man, whom God made in His own image, to whom He gave dominion over all other living things.

As to man's creation, Genesis gives a definite sequence of evolution. First, God formed the body of man out of the dust of the earth, from inanimate matter. Next He breathed the breath of Life into man's nostrils, and man became a living being. It was subsequently, after God had given man body and life, that man acquired understanding or intellect, the faculty of knowing good from evil, as God says, in Genesis.[1]

Except for the references to Divinity and good and evil, much of this might have come direct from a course on geologic history and natural evolution. The sequence of scientific evolution is given generally in this order: First gas, then water, dry land, plants, lower forms of life, higher forms of life, animals, and then man, the present crown and highest reach of the evolutionary process. This approximates the sequence of Genesis. As to man himself, the order of development is first the gross bodily form, next life, and finally mind, in both religion and science. These different stages did not occur instantly in man, but only after long periods of time.

In religion this process reflects an increasing consciousness, higher and higher existence. In man, the soul within him becomes more and more realized in the outer instruments of his being, as it rises to manifest God in the natural world.

Body came first to house life and mind. Body and life are not the same thing. As man is now constituted, life can expire from the body, leaving it lifeless. Similarly, life and mind are not the same thing. There are lower forms of life or one-celled organisms with little or no developed mind. The

[1] Genesis 3:22.

animals have only a rudimentary mind of instinct. Man has the mind of reason, the highest power of knowledge yet to appear in the evolution. Thus, all mind is not the same. Mind in various forms of life differs in size as well as in intellectual capacity. There are very low forms of mind, higher minds, animal mind and human mind. Even as to the rational mind of man, some people are far more rational than others. This means that some people are enlarging their mental faculty, while others remaining at lower levels, are barely rational and not much beyond the first level of reason attained long ago. The reasoning faculty itself is not new. It was reached far back in human history. The ancient Greeks, Hebrews, Hindus and Chinese all had highly rational and gifted men.

If there is to be a new forward step in evolution, clearly it will be for man to go higher than rationality. His new and higher mentality is to be as elevated above and different from the present human mind as man's mind is now above that of non-human life. To prepare for the change it is necessary to open ourselves to intuitional and other higher degrees of mind so that we can become ready for a supramental transformation, for the advent of a new power of knowledge in man. It is by such degrees, grades, and steps that all forward evolution has occurred in the past. The future can point in no other direction, and in this religion and science both agree. Both Christ and Paul were aware of this. Paul said to men, "Do not remain in the ignorance and futility of your minds; do not be babes in mind; have the mind of Christ, the mature wisdom of God."

"The foolishness of God," said Paul, "is higher than the wisdom of man." He meant that our present mind of reason, brilliant and remarkable as it is, and despite the great advances it has brought to man, is witless compared with the wisdom of God, the Higher Knowledge, the Mind of Christ, which humanity should next strive to attain. These things Christ and Paul knew long before modern science arose to trace the processes of evolution.

The mind of reason, as able and complex as it is, has not solved human problems, and cannot do so. The wisest among the statesmen admit this. They declare that, while better laws and improvements in social conditions are necessary and must be adopted, the laws and the institutions will fall short unless there is a change of human nature to a higher plane and a deeper insight. Law without Spirit is dead and creates nothing. The laws of the universe would be inert unless God moved in them and glorified their action. The civil rights crisis in our country is an example. Better civil rights laws are necessary and should and will be adopted, but without the change to a higher manhood, we will have the letter of the law but not the spirit of equality to which this country is dedicated.

Science, too, says that it will produce a man of higher mind, the mind of a computer. But man seeks to be not a machine but a Son of God. He seeks what Paul called *the mind of Christ,* what Aurobindo calls the super-mentality that knows without computation and endows man with direct, instant and full knowledge and vision of the Spirit. This is a knowledge that does not depend upon the laborious accumulation of phenomenal data or the tortuous and involved processes of logic.

Some people say, and quite in earnest, that they already have the mind of God. If this is so, we can see no evidence of it in the present conditions of the world and its recurrent chaos and threats of catastrophe. If it were so, man could scrap his battleships and send his armies home; but this cannot be so. Man is not God, and does not have God's mind. It is enough for man that he shall receive power to be the Son of God. Not even Christ said he was God, but the Son of God, and the Son of man. Is not Christ high enough for man?

We are, indeed, to go beyond the mind of reason, as has been said; but it is to attain the Christ-mind, the super-mentality. This will bring man to the threshold of union with God. Beyond that, beyond even the super-mentality, will be glory upon glory in the ineffable being and bliss of God, new heavens and a new earth, as Isaiah said, the "many mansions" of the house of God, where Christ went to prepare a place for us.

Let us not be dissuaded by those who say that they believe in perfection, yet that it cannot be, or that this is good but man and the world are not ready for it and never will be. The one-celled amoeba, when it was the highest form of life on earth, never dreamed or imagined that higher animal life would ever appear on earth, much less man. The animal could not conceive or foresee the appearance of present man. Shall present man ignore all that the history of religion and the records of science teach him, and preclude the possibility of his own further advance? Shall man be as blind to future change as the amoeba or the animal? Man is neither to regress nor to stand still, but to go forward and upward, sustained by the Divine arms in the glorious adventure of the soul in nature, as it ascends toward the bliss of the Divine.

It may be asked: Will this heightening of human consciousness, this new mentality, require for its evolution vast periods of geologic time, such as occurred in past evolutionary progression? Will it take millions of years? It should occur much quicker, even now; for evolutionary changes are occurring now more within man than in his outer physical form. In man's psychic or inner being, and his intellectuality, is the vast potential and assurance of victory and ascension to the Divine.

7

Thus the story of creation is far from ended. New chapters are to be added. Man himself is allowed by the Divine to be a participator in the creative process. This is true of no other life on earth. Man alone speculates concerning the creation of which he is a part. He is permitted to exercise a role in it by aspiring to a yet higher and Divine consciousness. Thus he not only changes himself, but assists in such a general change in humanity and in the world for the perfection of its institutions. Thus man in creative self-unfoldment are to become centers of Divine manifestation on earth, expressions of God in nature, the out-flowering of God in human existence.

Christ said, "If a son ask his father for bread will he give him a stone? Or if he asks for fish will he give him a serpent? Is God less than man that He should turn aside?" It is this bread of transformation, of purity, light, and power from above which we should ask of the Divine, having which we shall never hunger again. "I have meat that ye know not of," said Christ; "and this is the heavenly food we should seek." Paul said the creation waits with eager longing for the revealing of the Sons of God. The revealing of man the human, as man the Divine, is the aim of our creation and the goal of our evolution.

Thus men shall find glory and peace in the world. God's word spoken by Isaiah shall be fulfilled: "And men shall not hurt each other in all my holy mountain." And God will say of this, as He said in the beginning of Genesis, that He looked upon His work and found it good.

CHAPTER II

BODILY PERFECTION

BODILY PERFECTION

The state of perfection of any entity admits of no flaws in any of its constituent elements. Therefore, if man is to become perfect as a natural being, he must become perfect not only in mind and life, but also in body. All of these must manifest the inner, eternal perfection of the soul. There must be in the human being a mind of light, a life of purity, and a bodily excellence and beauty. Perfection of soul is to be expressed and made dynamic in perfection of mind, life and body. Only then can man be called perfect, as the Divine is perfect.

The body is not an island unto itself. It, too, is washed by the waves and the seas of our being. If the body is imperfect, the waves will cast its debris on the shores of all the continents of our self. If all is well with the body, it will ably support our mind, life and psychic being in the quest for the Divine. On the other hand, a fatigued or frequently ill body restrains us in this search.

Religion has always recognized that bodily condition affects spiritual development. A study of the scriptures and of the religions of the world will show that many or most of them contain dietary injunctions, rules of cleanliness, temperance, and so forth, as aids to the spiritual life.

Humanity intuitively understands the importance of bodily perfection. Athletics and sports contests fascinate the public and draw millions of people to witness them. There is a truth back of this absorption in the agility, grace, accuracy and fortitude displayed by athletes on the playing field, even though the contests are often and unnecessarily over-exaggerated, dangerous, brutalized and commercialized. People pay tribute to the strength, dexterity and stamina displayed by athletic contestants. They have done so since history began. Every civilization leaves a record of its athletics, just as it does of its religions, ethics, polity, art and other facets of its culture. The Olympic games of today are handed down to us from the ancient Greeks. The temples of ancient Indian cultures on the American continents had their ball-courts and athletic fields. No sooner are new athletic records set than men set out to break them. They must reach the poles of the earth and climb its highest mountains over and again. They train their bodies rigorously to be able to endure the Herculean strains of riding in space vehicles that orbit the earth, and the strange new physical environment of outer space, in preparation for projected journeys to other planets and the stars. What the body cannot now do physically, they demand that it learn to do.

Athletics help to develop cooperation with others, sportsmanship, the orderly discipline of accepting the decisions of an impartial arbiter, submission of self to a team effort, modesty in victory, and imperturbability in defeat. All of these are good attributes to cultivate for application to any other life activity. Even the spiritual seeker in his quest must learn to have skill, resourcefulness and courage, to be undisturbed by an occasional defeat on the path until he wins the highest crown of spiritual realization.

By this is not meant that you must rush out and become a ball-player or a mountain climber. What exercise you need, and the food, rest and care you require for your bodily health and strength, can be had without your becoming a champion athlete. What it does mean is that bodily perfection is an essential part of the integral perfection of mankind.

In at least one case, bodily perfection has actually been given a leading role in making spiritual attainment possible. This is the Hatha-Yoga of India. Where other religions promulgate a few simple rules for health, Hatha-Yoga has adopted an enormously complex and detailed system of involved and difficult acrobatic exercises for its devotees. It is that branch of Yoga which to most Westerners is known by such practices as standing on the head as a Yogic spiritual discipline. These exercises are not undertaken as a show, or for mere acrobatics, athletic skill, or health alone. The Hatha-Yoga performs these exercises daily to maintain his body in perfect physical condition and state of calm self-control so that he can receive the utmost in spiritual realization and peace, without being hindered by bodily weakness, illness, or disturbance.

Hatha-Yoga, like some other religions, tends to over-emphasize its particular path. Health is essential but exercises, strong muscles, and body suppleness will not, in themselves, make you spiritual. You need not indulge in such strenuous or involved exercises as Hatha-Yoga, or any other exhaustive physical system. That is why in India itself other systems of yoga, besides Hatha-Yoga exist, such as Raja-Yoga, Bhakti-Yoga and Karma-Yoga. I am not pointing this out to disparage Hatha-Yoga or exercise, but to show the extent to which bodily perfection has been recognized, even to an extreme degree, as necessary to spiritual attainment. Hatha-Yoga has at least served a useful purpose in stressing this necessity, and its best devotees recognize that it is not in itself the entire spiritual way.

In the West there are milder forms of religious participation in athletics. In this country, many religious denominations sponsor athletic programs, contests, and health centers. Religious schools and universities have such programs on a large scale. The government also encourages physical fitness.

In cases of extreme or partial physical impairment, we can do no work at all or do it not as well and for not as long, whether it be mental labor or otherwise. As we become stronger physically, we are better able to perform any duty or work, to stand the rigors of travel, exploration, or service to our country, in peace and war, and for every good cause. Christ was a sturdy carpenter. Moses lived to be 120, and to the end his eye was not dim nor his natural force abated. Buddha walked 17 miles a day from village to village, teaching as he went.

Up to this point we have largely been discussing the body as it now is; but the body has not reached the limit of its development. Just as there are higher levels of mind that man is seeking, so there are higher bodily levels to be reached. Beyond all of this is the ascent to the ultimate height of spiritual being. In this ascent the body is to be included. The rise in consciousness is also to take place in the body for its perfection. There will be a spiritual and mental excellence in the body as well as a physical excellence. As man becomes more spiritual, the body must become a fit support for the spiritual and infused with its light and power. As the body now is the physical support of mental man, it must become the support of spiritual law. The body thus will become a conscious instrument of the spirit and is to evidence its power and perfection.

As the body grows in perfection, its power and its response and service to the spirit must increase. At the same time the power of the spirit over the body will grow. Here we will observe a dual process. The body becomes more able to serve the spirit, and the power of the spirit over the body becomes fully established. This cannot occur without an integral transformation of mind, life and body itself. Only then will we no longer be forced to declare, as the Bible says, that the spirit is willing but the flesh is weak. In the man of the time of the Bible, the flesh was weak, but it is our goal that the flesh should become strong and perfect, and that is the aim of the Bible for the body of man. Such is the aim of our evolution. Without this entire transformation of ourselves, the Divine life on earth in all its fullness cannot occur. The body is not to be a lame and weak member if man is to be perfect, as Christ said that he should be.

In transformation the body is a participator and an agency. We should not consider that the body is incapable of such a high role. The body already has its mentality and will. It operates our involuntary nervous systems, whether we are awake or asleep. It conducts millions of involved processes of an infinite exactitude in keeping our bodily organism intact and functioning. It directs our breathing and heartbeats, rushes to heal our wounds when we are injured, and to cure our illnesses when we are sick. Thus the body already has a consciousness. In the transformation this bodily consciousness will be heightened. It is to receive the light, joy and power from above, but it also is to fulfill its conscious role in its own perfection. The consent and will of the body are required for this change in itself. It is not to be reluctantly dragged or inhibited to perfection.

It is for a great purpose that perfection of the body is to occur. If man can bring the spiritual power into the materiality, into the body his long-cherished dream of perfectibility of the human race, perfection of the individual and society could be attained. An inner mastery of self and a full mastery, control, and utilization of nature could at last become possible. These are the conditions for a divine life, and the Kingdom of Heaven on earth. Man shall not enter the kingdom as a disembodied spirit or an abstract mentality, but with the body as a glorious manifestation of his existence. We are not to offer at the Divine altar a naked spirit, but one clothed and adorned with a perfect and immortal body.

The body has already manifested mind and life within its physical structure. That is, the body houses both our mind and our life-energies. Both act from within the body. This is clear. Now what is the next step? The body has already manifested mind and life. We think and we act. What is the body to manifest next?

We know that the body also houses the soul for, as Paul says, "You are the temple of God; the spirit of God dwells within you." The next step is for the body to manifest the spirit, the supreme light and power of the Soul within. If the body can do that, it would cast off from its earthly frame all that makes it imperfect and mortal. We would then become, as Paul predicted, manifested Sons of God. For the body to manifest the soul is, therefore, the ultimate goal in man's upward evolution. The health, strength and existence of the body would then be maintained in perfection by its spiritual inhabitant. The spirit would not only be within, but without, in the individual and in the world. As Paul said, "Know ye not that your body is the temple of the Holy Spirit?" Therefore, glorify God in your body as well as in your spirit. The perfection thus attained by the body will house and support the perfection of mind and life, of our entire being. The perfection of the body is the last and most difficult step of our progress. It is the final and ultimate condition for the divine existence of man. It is the crowning achievement in the transcending of imperfection. It is the conquest of death. In the words of the Apostle Paul, "The last enemy, Death, shall be conquered."

As this perfection occurs, the body will take on a capacity and ability to act for the purpose of the soul, far in excess of the body's present range of powers. The body could acquire a marvelous beauty and an indefatigable strength. It would reflect the splendor of the spirit within it, and cast about it an illumination from its eternal inner flame. Such would be the body into which the spiritual consciousness has descended for a total perfection. Even now, individuals who have made some degree of spiritual progress have an aura and appearance which beautifies them beyond others, and imparts to them a warmth which irresistibly draws other persons toward them to learn the secret and bliss of transformation. Bodily perfection is not to occur overnight for the human race, but the way is open if we call to the Divine for it to transpire.

The Divine will descend to transform materiality and our very bodies as the summit of our ascending evolution. Such will be the supreme perfection of the body. Isaiah says of God: "Behold, I create new heavens and a new earth . . . be ye glad and rejoice forever in that which I create."[1] In this new earth shall there not be a new and perfect manhood to be glad and rejoice forever? "If Christ ascended," said the Apostle Paul, "he also descended." By that descent the bodily manifestation will acquire a beauty and radiance that we cannot now imagine. As the New Testament says, "We do not know what we shall be like, but we shall know Him when He comes, for we shall be like unto Him."

---

[1]Isaiah 65:17-18.

CHAPTER III

PEACE OF LIFE

PEACE OF LIFE

Much has been written in recent years on peace of mind and peace of soul. Books and numerous articles have been published on these subjects, some written by religious teachers and some by psychologists. But little has been written on peace of life and how to attain it. Yet surely it is obvious that more than the mind in us must be peaceful. In fact, peace of mind is often taught and advocated in order to bring peace into other parts of the being, to the body and the nerves.

Yet without peace in the life itself, in the will, the emotions, the life energies that course like invisible currents in our body, there can be no quiet and no fulfillment of spiritual realization. Therefore it is not enough that there be peace in the mind. It is not enough moreover to feel the assurance that there is eternal peace in the soul. Another conquest is required. This is to find the secret way to peace in the will, emotional, vital, energetic plane of our being.

If I cannot engage in the varied activities of life, if I cannot perform my useful work in the world without nervously, excitedly, miserably or violently losing my peace of mind and violating every dictate of the soul, I have attained no satisfactory peace of my being. I would be still far from equanimity. I would be still poisoned by the venom of turbid emotions and spoiled actions.

So in this chapter we shall discuss peace in our lives, not as an abstract mental concept or something apart and removed in a supposedly disembodied soul but as a present and actual reality, something to be treated separately from the problem of peace of mind. The mind must be quiet, but the life also must be calm. It must have that peace which will enable us to live in harmony and happiness.

It is necessary for the divine consciousness to descend into us and to emerge from within us in order to attain perfection and liberation, conscious union with the Divine. But it is important to remember that this descent of the force above must permeate not only our minds and bodies but the vital instrumentalities, the will, the emotions. That is what we are stressing here. The divine descent and the changes it can effect must be in these active instrumentalities as well. Not only my mind buy my will, my nerves must be transformed, and it is not the mind which will transform them but the divine force. If the higher consciousness descends into the mind only it may bring peace of soul, deliverance, and possibly knowledge. But it is only when the divine force comes into the will, the emotions, that the actual realization of peace in our lives becomes a living reality.

Then we not only understand peace and know its origin but experience it. We may gain a high degree of knowledge, we may have occasional glimpses of peace in the soul, even some partial vistas of mystic spiritual experiences. But if we cannot calm our vital will, and energies, if we cannot control our passions and the spasmodic leaping of the emotions, we cannot have peace of life.

I am sure that this is obvious to all. We may gain and hold a strong faith and a satisfying intellectual concept concerning the spiritual life. But at the same time our life, emotions, and will may make a mockery of all the ground we have won. As a result we may backslide too frequently, gain steps only to feel we have lost them. We may become discouraged or depressed. Everyone who seeks to follow the spiritual path goes through these trials. To succeed in overcoming such trials it is necessary first to comprehend that it is the life force with which we are mainly contending.

The mind is difficult enough to quiet. Day and night it rattles on, even in sleep. Yet the life is even a harder problem. Life says to mind: go right ahead, reason to the top of your bent, spin out your logical conclusions, but I shall have my way. Even if mind tells me to beware I shall fling its caution to the wind and gratify my vital desires. I will revive old burning and searing memories, and hover narcissistically over my ego, fondling and mollifying it as if neither reason, heart, nor soul exist. Now what happens to us as a result of this life rebellion? If it is not subdued, we can neither act rightly nor live calmly. The great apostle to the Gentiles, Paul, had a deep perception of this problem, and spoke of it in his letter to the Romans in these words: "But I see another law in my members warring against the law of my mind, and bringing me into captivity to the law of sin which is in my members."[1] If we substitute the word ignorance for Paul's word sin we have the same connotation.

As for faith, says the vital or life part of us, it must surrender to me exactly what I want on my terms, or I will count it a cheat and a counterfeit. Religion must give me what I want or I will find wrong enough with religion. I will complain to God that I have been rebuked without cause and denied what my ego seeks. My faith will be faith only when every desire of my life is granted. When it is otherwise, says life, then faith becomes doubt to me. I will be faithful only for a price.

So far as life is concerned, faith can be a traitor and intellect a fool. The Book of Job in the Bible is centered around this problem of how to meet life in pleasure and pain, how to bring life under the divine transformation. According to the Bible a conversation was held between God and Satan. Satan said to God: "Job only serves you because you bless him. You have a wall of protection around him. Let me penetrate that wall and afflict him; let me torment him, take away his material possessions, and he will turn and curse you." Satan miscalculated Job, who stood firm in his life, and in his devotion to God, and we must learn to do the same.

How then is the transformation of life to be effected? It is important to know how to do this because there must be peace in all parts of our being. All must be brought into harmony with each other in order to perfect our existence. There must be peace in life, mind, body, manifesting the peace of the soul. All the members of our being must be perfected within themselves and in relation to each other, and in respect to the function each performs.

As Paul says further in The First Letter to the Corinthians: "But now hath God set the members everyone of them in the body as it has pleased him and if they were all one member, where should the body be? But now are they many members but one body. And the eye cannot say unto the hand I have no need of thee: nor again the head to the feet I have no need of you. Nay, much more these members of the body which seem to be more feeble are necessary . . . that there should be no schism in the body but that the members should have the same care for one another. And when one member suffers all the members suffer with it; or one member be honored, all the

---

[1] Romans 7:24

21

members rejoice with it.''[2]

Now all the members of our being as Paul said, must honor, rejoice and strengthen each other. In order to understand clearly the relationship of the life factor to the other members of our being, let us consider the order in which each of them developed in evolutionary process. First there was matter, the rocks, the dust of the earth, the elements, the inconscient materiality that is present as the base of our physique today. Next, life emerged on the evolutionary scene, simple and rude in form at first and barely conscient, then progressing to the complexity of the animal. Next, the human emerged with the reasoning mind, along with refinements in form corresponding with a rise in the level of consciousness.

Now the mind is the highest power of present mankind as well as of the entire evolutionary process up to this era. We rely on the reasoning mind to direct, control, and organize our lives, therefore we tend to believe that the mind is master and can solve our problems. We seem to think that if we can only get peace and contentment in our mind, the earlier parts of our being which preceded it in the evolutionary scale, that is body and life, can be satisfactorily regulated by the mind.

But in practice we find this is not the case. Too often the mind instead of being the controller and organizer looks around frantically for something, anything that can control it and regulate its own disorder. The offices of psychiatrists are filled with people in this dilemma. As the Buddhists said thousands of years ago, the mind must be controlled like a monkey on a string. It is like a fly that takes its food from your dining room table or from the garbage can, like a flea that hops from one thing to another. So the mind of itself cannot solve the problem of peace of life.

The mind itself must be quieted by bringing into it the divine force, the supramental light, the power and purity of the infinite. The mind can then be of help while not the final means of quieting the life. The mind must surrender itself to the higher spiritual consciousness. But this alone will not suffice. The life, the will, the emotions must make the same surrender to the Divine, as Paul says, ''Much more for the members of the body which seem to be feeble.''

The divine descent must come into the life and will also as a province different from the mind, a province of our entire being but retaining as it were its own autonomy and freedom of action. The vital life forces will not

---

[2] I Corinthians 12:18-26.

submit to being suppressed or browbeaten by the mind but must find their own transformation. The vital, the will, the emotional, the life must surrender itself to God and worship and serve the Divine just as the mind and heart surrender themselves. If you will think about it in this way, if you say to yourself, my will, my life energy, my emotions are dedicated to the Divine, then the peace of God will descend not just into your mind and heart as Paul says in the Philippians, but into your life also. Then you will stop the constant war between the mind and the life, and there will be peace between and within them.

If we doubt this autonomy of life, if we hesitate to put any stock in its enormous power, then we are overlooking the realities of existence and all evolutionary factuality. When life came upon the scene it had to fend for itself, get food, find protection and security, reproduce, satisfy the demands that would keep the life going in itself and its posterity. Does anyone imagine that these powerful forces are not still active in us today, or left no imprint on our existence? The latecomer, mind, which developed after life, can aid in making the life less ego-centric, more inclined toward general as well as individual well-being and happiness. But it is only when this life force itself is transformed and consecrated to the Divine that we are liberated. Indeed, the most difficult step of individual liberation is the transformation of life-activities, will, and emotions.

But when this life transformation is finally achieved we will then refer all of our action to the Divine, asking for divine guidance in what to do and how to do all of our deeds. All fears and frustrations will then depart from us. We will then have that renunciation which the Gita says alone brings peace and satisfaction. For we have then given up the fruits of our actions, the egoistic engrossment in results, return, or rewards. What we then do in our lives is done for the Divine, for His truth, purpose, love and joy in our lives and in the lives of all, in the cosmos and beyond it to the ineffable reaches of the infinite.

We have pointed out that the mind cannot effect this transformation in our lives. Indeed we must be alert that the mind with its ignorance and limitation does not throw us off the track. The mind of man is not yet the mind of light which it will be when it is transformed by the divine force as the life must be transformed. Mind and life as well as the body fall under this law and principle.

If we keep ourselves open to that divine force there occurs at last the conversion in the twinkling of an eye, *in such an hour as we think not*. As an ancient Buddhist saying goes, we may be ignorant in one moment and a Buddha the next if only we allow the Divine to take up the burden of this life

23

0245863

transformation for us, and persist through all trials. Offer to God the very smallest cells and elements of your nervous and emotional being and will until they too are illumined with the divine light, charged with its power, happy with its joy, calm with its detachment, praying, worshiping and rejoicing in the Divine with the rest of your being. Face all difficulties with a calm mind, a dauntless courage, and an unshakeable reliance on the Divine. Be patient and persistent, more persistent than adverse forces or circumstances. Then you will succeed, for there is no failure to a person who is sincere and constant in their spiritual search. Then will we truly love the Lord our God with all our mind, all our heart, all our soul, and all of our life.

CHAPTER IV

THE REMOVAL OF THE EGO

THE REMOVAL OF THE EGO

The current view of the ego seems to be that it is an undesirable slant of human character, or an inescapable entity of the psychological structure of man. It is undesirable, but it is not inescapable. The term "egotistic" is taken to mean self-centeredness. That is how the ego originated. It was a center of self, the original focus or gathering-point of human consciousness in the beginning of the evolution of the race. This was a vast step forward out of inconscient life. The individual appeared on the life scene as the key to the evolutionary advance and to the future of man.

Nevertheless, like most beginnings or initiations, the ego was crude then and it remains crude now. The ego was the center around which the I, or the me, was first established, but it was not established to remain in its pristine crudity. Vast forward steps were next to be taken from the ego itself to a yet higher consciousness, to a loftier individuality. The ego was a step forward in order that there might be subsequaent and greater steps forward from the ego itself. Man should not underrate the role that the ego has played in the past, nor permit himself to be ruled by it any longer. He now has or is developing a larger and expanded consciousness by which to govern his existence.

The ego brought man out of a diffusion or conglomerate, a mass of amorphos and indistinguishable life, a mere coral reef on the seashore of existence. It gave us certain characetristics of uniqueness different from those of others. It equipped us with the motivation and the will to survive and prosper in the face of all opposition and difficulties, traits which directed to a higher purpose serve us well to this day. The ego could be primitively hostile, savage, and selfish, but it was intent in preserving the first germ of individuality which it represented and from which would grow human centers of divine consciousness in whom savagery and hostility could be eliminated. The savage of the ego was to become the saint of the soul.

Now the purposes that the ego served in man's evolutionary past are over and finished. For man to progress further, the ego must be removed from his being. The ego is an anachronistic and vestigial in man's consiousness today as the appendix is in the body. There is no longer any use for either; whatever useful purpose either served in the past no longer exists. The appendix can be easily removed from the body by a surgical operation if it gives trouble, as it sometimes does; but to remove the ego, which always gives trouble, requires a psychic operation which is not easy, but very difficult.

Why is this the case? It is because, as we have seen, the ego is our first and oldest focus of consciousness. It was there in the beginning. It is long-established and entrenched, and consequently hard to get out. It is like a hostile army in a strong position. It has no intention to strike its flag and surrender unconditionally. It is accustomed to hold empire over all of our being, and will not give up its prerogatives without a fight. To overcome it is a struggle, but a struggle that can be won.

The first step in removing the ego is to realize that it must be eradicated entirely. Our being must be freed from even subtle or disguised aspects or remnants of it. The ego must not be allowed to build up or enlarge itself in other directions or to hide under other appearances. The ego of family, race, or religion, for instance, is not to be substituted for the individual ego. It should not be permitted to glorify or extenuate itself as then being of a wider nature and resting on a broader base. Such an extended ego is a more serious obstacle because it is a multiplication of indivdual ego and gathers strength from numbers. The group ego has all the drawbacks of the individual ego, plus more power. An individual is frequently more hesitant to disregard the group ego than their own ego. They are reluctant to go against what the group may consider to be its interest, but is really not good for it. An example is race prejudice, which is bad; but members of the prejudiced group often hesitate to speak out against it even if they realize it is bad. In government, totalitarianism is a form of group ego.

The ego is separative. It is so even if transpsosed to a group. If it is family ego, or religious or race ego, for example, it separates itself from other families, religious, and races in sympathy and in aims.

The next step in removing the ego is to replace it with a higher consciousness. This is our true being, the soul. The true being in us is individual, yet one with all others and with the Divine. It is not separative like the ego, which is united with neither God nor other men. The ego is individual and separative, while the soul is individual and uniting.

We must beware of the stratagems and tricks of the ego within us. When it is utterly defeated and cast down it will call on others and on God for help, but only until the crisis is past. Then before we know it, the ego has crept again into an arrogant predominace over our lives. In its conceit, it thinks itself secure against future falls. Pride, says the Bible, goes before a fall, and pride is the parade of the ego.

In dissolving the ego, it is necessary to observe how it permeates our thoughts, speech and actions, like a grey fog that clings to everything. We should see the falsity and damage of egoism, the the harm that it does to us and others, the wounds that it inflicts, and how ridiculous it is. Is it not absurd that we should harbor anything so injurious to us? We can smile at our oversight and resolve to banish this absurdity. We should withhold all sanction from the ego, rule it out on every occasion. The ego will finally loose its hold on us when we are in oneness at all times. The meat on which this Ceasar feeds is the separative desires of the ego.

The ego cannot be dispelled in us by waving a wand or giving a command. Time is necessary to drive it out. Observe calmly how far you have progressed, and what remains to be done. Watch for the weak points in your nature and the occasions and situations in which you have been prone to yield to ego, and make the required corrections. You must exert a constant vigilant pressure against the ego until you have loosened the last of its tentacles. One by one they will lose their hold until your inner being can easily throw off its last feeble clutches, and you are free.

Do not be dismayed if the ego crops up again in you unexpectedly, and you have a momentary fall from which you recover. This is a good sign and not a bad one. It signifies that you have recognized ego-centricity in yourself. This is a skirmish won over the foe. Many people are oblivious of their egoism, and are so deluded as to think their actions commendable. They live in an upside-down world in which the ego is above, the soul below. They do not even know they have egoism, much less how to throw it out. So you have gained ground when you can see egoism in yourself, for then you can start to get rid of it. Thereafter, it is only a question of time and the right methods.

Egoistic people speak egoistic language; the "I" and the "my" interlard their speech. It is "my" this, "my" that, "my" advance, "my" demonstration, "my" success, "my" realization, "my" *everything*. Perhaps even after we have recognized the ego in us, and determined to dissolve it, we may find ourselves prone to continue thinking and saying these things. "The remedy," says Aurobindo, "is to think constantly of the Divine, not of one's self, to work, act, (and carry on your spiritual devotions) for the Divine; not to consider how this or that affects me personally, not to claim anything, but to refer all to the Divine. It will take time to do that sincerely and thoroughly, but it is the proper way. The ego-centric man feels and takes things as they affect him. Does this please me or displease, give me gladness or pain, flatter my pride, vanity or ambitions or hurt them, satisfy my desires or thwart them. The unegoistic man does not look at things like that. He looks to see what things are in themselves or would be if he were not there, what is their meaning, how they fit into the scheme of things — or else, he feels calm and equal and refers all to the Divine. Or if he is a man of actions, how they will serve the work that has to be done or the life of the world or the cause he serves, etc. There can be many points of view which are not ego-centric." [1]

Nowhere are the subtle masks and disguises of egoism more to be guarded against than in the high virtues such as ethicism and religious practice. Here they can engender the most severe fall. They take forms such as self-righteousness and self-satisfaction. Those subject to such vanity want to be known as renowned disciples, leaders of the elect, lieutenants of the prophets. Even if they subdue these feelings they may be crushed by the failure of their noble ethical ideals or religious aims because they have not put this last refinement of ambition from them. They may believe that they can act as they see fit, and that they are the instruments of God in so doing. Chirst refers to such individuals as hypocrites who make broad their phylacteries, seek the chief seats in the synagogue, and for a pretense, make long prayer; "Therefore," he said, "they shall receive the greater damnation. They seek only to have men hail them in the streets, saying 'Rabbi, Rabbi'."

The signs of egoism are many. Among them are outbursts of anger or vehement expression. Science says that these excitements dangerously over-load our physical systems and organs with hormones and secretions, and take away the essential electrical polarizarion of the bodily cells, all of which harms our health. Egoism and bad health are often companions. As we progress, we shall be able to control these outbursts and have good health in addition to serenity.

---

[1] Sri Aurobindo, *Letters of Sri Aurobindo,* 4th Series (Pondicherry: Sri Aurobindo Ashram Press, 1961) pp. 431-432.

As Aurobindo further says, "When one has a wider consciousness, one knows that each one has his own way of looking at things and finds in that way his own justification, so that both parties in a quarrel believe themselves to be in the right. It is only when one looks from above in a consciousness clear of ego that one sees all sides of a thing and also their real truth." [2]

Another sign of the ego is the tendency to be always telling of the real or imaginary faults of other people. This itself is the worst of faults. The ego cannot judge others, for it sees all through its own distorted lenses, and never in the right view or the right spirit. It is only the calm, disinterested, dispassionate, all-compassionate and all-loving spirit that can judge and see rightly the strength and the weakness in each being." [3]

We also must watch for the specious philosophies of the ego. These center in the mind precisely because it can argue and propose logic and theory in the support of egoism as a way of life, everything from "Eat, drink and be merry, for tomorrow I may die," to a defense of egoism as enlightened self-interest. The argument for enlightened self-interest runs like this: My self-interest, my very egoism for its own protection, requires me not to take undue advantage of you. I will be wary of injuring you, not because I have love for you, but because you will retaliate against me or not favor me otherwise. In other words, I must be fair to you out of fear. The results of this theory are always somehow less than enlightened. It looks on man not as a brother but as an actual potential enemy. Inevitably, one self-interest climbs over another and things are no better. It is a mock ethicism and a spurious religion that is responsible for many of the world's ills. It is right to do unto others as you would have them do unto you, and this principle is taught by nearly all religions; but it is right because it is a spiritual law and not a theory of the the human ego. As Christ said, When you give a dinner or a banquet, do not invite your friends or your kinsmen or rich neighbors, lest they invite you also in return and you be repaid. But when you give a feast invite the poor, the maimed, the lame, the blind, and you will be blessed, because they cannot repay you; you will be repaid at the resurrection of the just. [4]

The ego cannot drive itself out. The physical ego cannot drive egoism out of physical impulses. The emotional ego cannot drive egosim out of physical impulses. The emotional ego cannot drive egoism out of passions.

---

[2] Sir Aurobindo, *Letters of Sri Aurobindo,* 4th Series (Pondicherry: Sir Aurobindo Ashram Press, 1961) p. 435

[3] Ibid. p. 436.

[4] Luke 14:12-14.

The mental ego cannot drive egoism out of the thoughts. If you can dispel it from the mind you can move more readily to dispel it from the rest of yourself, for this is the seat of its self-justification.

How is mental egoism overcome? You can poise yourself above the maelstrom and rapids of your thoughts. For this purpose the mind can be divided into two parts: one produces thoughts constantly and organizes and controls our activities; the other is the witness and will that presides over the thoughts themselves. It monitors the mind and does not accept all the output of the thought machinery. It exercises supervision and choice over the thinking faculty whose function is to think for man and not to will for him; the will is above the mind, and above the will is the Divine. Some thoughts this witness calls or rejects, others it modifies or corrects. It is the ruler in the house of the mind, and master of its domain. It was before the ego and will be after it. In this witness is the psychic fire of the soul that burns away all the dross of egoism in the thoughts and leaves them pure and immaculate.

Let us realize that the ego must be dissolved; take the steps necessary to remove it, and call on the Divine Force to effect this transformation in our nature. We need not be impatient at the time required, or despondent because of difficulties encountered, for this liberation is to be ours. As Paul wrote to the Corinthians: "The Lord knows that the thoughts of the wise are futile. For all things are yours . . . whether present or future: All are yours; and you are Christ's and Christ's is God's."

CHAPTER V

PSYCHIC SILENCE

PSYCHIC SILENCE

Silence is both physical and psychic. By physical silence is meant cessation of sounds ordinarily discernible to the human ear. By psychic silence is meant a mental and inner quiet. We make ourselves silent in order to hear a distant sound in the atmosphere. So also we become silent in our minds to hear the voice of God. We fall silent to listen to man whom we see, and to God whom we do not see.

We may believe that we are in physical silence, but there are all the time sounds of higher frequency, pitch, or vibration that man's ear cannot detect. The sharper ears of the animal often hear what we miss. But if in the evolution man has lost ground to the animal in physical hearing, he has gone far beyond the animal in psychic hearing and in the faculty of psychic silence.

Thus Moses in the silence of the desert saw the burning bush that was yet not consumed and heard the voice of God commanding him to lead the enslaved Hebrews from Egypt to the freedom of the Promised Land. Thus Mohammed heard a voice commanding him to write the Koran and stepped out of the cave in which he was meditating to look into the great eyes of the angel Gabriel. Moses and Mohammed both had a psychic hearing sharper than that of their contemporaries, and could hear in the divine silence what other men missed.

Physical silence has always been extolled by religion. James says in

The New Consciousness

the New Testament that the tongue no man can tame; it is an unruly evil, full of deadly poison.[1] In the Talmud, one of the ancient rabbis says: All my days I have grown up amongst the wise and I have found nought of better service than silence. Not learning but doing is the chief thing, and who so is profuse of words causes sin. Religion is full of such exegetics on the virtue of silence. There is a time to keep silence and a time to speak, says Ecclesiastes.[2] It is right to be silent before one on whom wise words will be wasted; it is a mistake to keep silent before one who thirsts for wisdom.

If religion extols physical silence, it praises psychic silence even more. One of the world religions, Buddhism, has as it ultimate aim the silence of the void, annihilation of self, absorption in nirvana. Here is neither God nor soul; the dewdrop slips into the shining sea of non-existence, utter silence and void. What could cause such an overwhelming emphasis on the silence? It is easy to explain its fascination and why it won and still holds hundreds of millions of adherents in the orient. Under Buddhism the world and men are an illusion like the trick of a magician or the flickering of a silent motion picture. They are no more real, in the Buddhist phrase, than the horns of a rabbit or a barren woman's child. By denying the reality of existence the Buddhists attain a great if negative peace. All pain and sorrow disappear because there is no existence in which they can be suffered. The problems of life are over for the ego; it has vanished. Keep the mind empty, tranquil, selfless, says a Buddhist scripture. We should even be silent about the silence, for silence in itself is not a reality but the void. How can one speak of the void?

Thus Buddha made a religion of the silence. But this is only a partial truth. In his zeal for the silence and his distaste for outer religious cere-monies, Buddha over-emphasized the silence and compartmentalized the Divine to exclude all except silence. The Buddhists themselves have found this impracticable. They cannot live by it. Like other people they find that the problems of life are real and that they must act to solve them. God is silent but He also speaks. He is passive and detached, yet also active and involved, and real in both aspects. Like the cloud in the sky that passes silently overhead, it has the potential of the world-shaking storm, the torren-tial rain, the fierce hurricane of the wind, the power of the lightning, and the peal of distant thunder.

Nevertheless, mankind owes Buddha much for teaching the silent

---

[1] James 3:8.
[2] Ecclesiastes 3:7.

side of the divine truth. For this he deserves the avatarhood which men attribute to him. If he over-stressed silence this is no different from the way that some earnest Christians over-stress love. Such Christians say that God is love, and that is all and the sum of truth and religion. The Bible makes no such statement. The Bible in one place says that God is love but in other verses it says that He is just, righteous, merciful, beautiful, and holy. Are we forced to single out any one of these and confine God to it if we could? Is God not infinite and beyond limitation whether by Buddhists, Christians, or others? Does not God include everything we would take from Him, and all that we cannot see in Him? Is not human intelligence, poor in content and partisan in outlook when compared with Divine intelligence?

Common sense must be used. When we say of a human friend, "he is kind," that does not mean that he may not be at the same time courageous, tactful, loyal, and wise. He is a much more valuable friend if he is all those things in addition to being kind. It is wonderful that God is love, but it is also wonderful that He has in addition the power, the will, and the divine intelligence to make His love effective. How could He answer our prayers otherwise? If I have love for you but no way or will to respond to your need or distress, what kind of love is that? God is the divine friend who watches over us tenderly and delivers us from evil. He not only loves us, but with a mighty arm thwarts and destroys those who would injure us and attempt to cast into shadow the progress of the human race. The natural thunder of the storm is nothing compared with the sound of God's mighty voice against the evil, the unjust, and the tyrannical and the anti-christs of any age. It was for this that David prayed in the 83rd Psalm: "Keep not thy silence, O God: hold not thy peace and, be not still, O God, for lo thine enemies make a tumult."[3] God is more than silent and loving. He is also the mighty victor crowned with laurels. He dispels the dark forces which try to defeat the noblest of our kind who lead and inspire man in his march toward a divine peace and immortal destiny.

Now that we have placed the silence in its proper perspective, let us see how to obtain it. The easiest way is to bring it down from above, but this requires a total dedication on the part of the individual. If we stop a moment to consider we will perceive that silence is our main path to the Divine. We live in silent reliance on God. In the most serious, portentous, perilous moments of life, we pray silently to the Divine from the secret recesses of the heart.

---

[3] Psalm 83:1-2.

"Go into your room", said Christ", and pray to the Father which is in secret and thy Father which seeth in secret shall reward thee openly."[4] Aspire to bring down the silence of God just as you aspire to call down His power and light into your being. The silence from above will enable you to be calm, detached, impersonal and impartial as God is. You will have this calm in your activities, just as God is calm and detached in His activities which are on a scale far vaster than yours. Do not fear that you will be unable to act. It is the man with the silent, calm mind, and not the noisy, turbulent mind, who has the best judgment and the genius and will to do the right thing at the right time. "Which of you," said Christ, "by taking thought can add a cubit to his stature? Of myself I do nothing," He said, "it is the Father within me who doeth the work." Christ was the witness and not the worker. In that sense Christ Himself was silent and did nothing.

Aurobindo describes how he silenced his mind through instructions he received from a Hindu yogi named Lele. "It was my great debt to Lele that he showed me this: 'Sit in meditation, but do not think, only look at your mind; you will see thoughts coming into it, before they can enter, throw them away from your mind 'til your mind is capable of entire silence.'

"I had never heard before of thought coming visibly into the mind from the outside," said Aurobindo, "but I did not think either of questioning the truth or the possibility, I simply sat down and did it. In a moment my mind became silent as a windless air on a high mountain summit and then I saw one thought and then another coming in a concrete way from the out-side. I flung them away before they could enter and take hold of the brain and in three days I was free. From that moment, in principle, the mental being in me became a free intelligence, a universal mind, not limited to the narrow circle of personal thought as a laborer in a thought factory. But a receiver of knowledge from all the hundred realms of being and free to choose what it willed in the vast sight-empire and thought empire."[5]

Science also has seen the necessity of inner silence. Its response has been to create the techiques of psychoanalysis. By these techniques science tries to bring quiet and calm into disturbed thoughts and emotions. But it has not preempted the field, or replaced the spiritual insight which saw the need of silence millenniums before Freud was born in the late nineteenth century.

The spiritual approach to the achievement of silence and that of

---

[4] Matthew 6:6.
[5] Sri Aurobindo, *On Yoga II,* Tome 2, pp. 359-360.

psychoanalysis are different. The spiritual throws away the thoughts; psychoanalysis lets them in for analyzing. Under the spiritual method the disturbing thoughts do not get in to disturb. Under psychoanalysis they not only get in but are invited. It is like opening the gate of the fortress to the enemy when you could keep him out. The psychologist opens the gate to the foe and then tries to fight him when he is already within the walls. It is much easier to keep these hostile legions out than to disarm them in your own territory.

The psychologist urges the patient to pull out for examination every shred of thought no matter how base, sordid, low or degraded. He believes that in that way he can find the clue to the trouble of the patient and cure him. But it is not necessary to be a trained psychologist to understand that this process is a terrifying and often a revolting experience. Psychologists themselves admit that it is often as hard on the patient as the problem which caused him to consult the psychologist in the first place. It is an old proverb that confession is good for the soul, but better than confession is silent mastery over yourself and your thoughts. You will then have no sins to pour out in agony before others. They will be burnt to ashes by the soul on the altar of the Divine.

The psychologist says that by his analysis he can uncover suppressed thoughts lying dormant in the subconscious and compulsively rising in distorted dreams and unfortunate or tragic actions. But the spiritual method is more direct and effective. Since the spiritual throws the thoughts away before they can get in, they can neither enter the conscious nor sink into the subconscious. They are not there at all.

The science of psychology too often operates like an elevator that runs in only one direction, to the basement and the cellar. It goes down to the dankest and darkest layers of the lower consciousness and motives. It seldom rises upward to the super-conscious of divine light within and above us. It was for this reason that Christ said: "I am from above and you are from below." He said in effect I am not of the world of your thoughts but above them. And the Scripture says that many believed him.[6]

This does not mean to imply that the science of psychology cannot be helpful. What is objectionable is that some psychologists like some doctors do not concede the superior role of the spiritual in all healing, whether it be in physical or psychological illness; or he attempts to supersede the spiritual,

---

[6] John 8:23-30.

minimizes it, or merely tolerates it as of no practical help to his patient in freeing the mind as Aurobindo said his mind became free.

There are, of course, psychologists, just as there are doctors, who give full credit to the spiritual influence in healing and rely on it. For instance, the late Carl Jung, who with Freud and Adler was a co-founder of modern psychology, said that among all the patients he had psychoanalyzed, he had never effected a permanent cure in any patient who did not take a turn to the spiritual. In this approach there is a proper conciliation between the spiritual and psychoanalysis in bringing peace and quiet to the disturbed and alleviating their inner misery and turmoil.

Do not be fearful that because you are silent within you will be an automaton or an imbecile without. It is a common saying that still water runs deep; it has a reservoir of power.

There is a story of a sage to whom a man went for instruction. The man asked the sage: "How can I become spiritual?" The sage replied: "Make your mind quiet." The man did so and rushed back to the sage and said, "My brain is empty of thought, I cannot think, I am becoming an idiot." When the man had left, the sage said: "How can he become an idiot if he is one already?" The trouble was that the man did not pause to see where the thoughts he was uttering were coming from. Instead of flinging out the thought he was busy thinking what an idiot he was becoming. "So," said the sage, "I dropped him and his precious silence, as I was not very patient in those days."

An ancient folk-lore story on silence and how it can be misconstrued is the story of the two monks. One was a wandering monk who stopped at a monastery to rest. He was welcomed by a one-eyed monk who lived there. They sat down together to enter into the dialogue of silence. Presently the visiting monk raised one finger. The monastery monk then raised two fingers. The visiting monk then raised three fingers. At this, the one-eyed monk stood up and shook his fist at the visiting monk then ran out of the room. The visiting monk got up to leave. As he was departing, the superior of the monastery met him and asked why he was going away so soon. The visitor said, "We were in a dialogue of silence, and I raised one finger meaning Budda is one. He raised two fingers meaning there is also the law which makes two. I then raised three fingers including the brotherhood, whereupon he clenched his fist, meaning all of these are combined in one. He outdid me in the dialogue, so I am leaving." With that the visitor departed and the one-eyed monk burst into the room with a club in his hand.

"Why is this?" asked the superior. "He raised one finger at me," said the monk, "meaning you have only one eye. I raised two fingers graciously recognizing that he had two eyes. He was not satisfied at this, but then raised three fingers to further insult me, meaning that together we have three eyes. I could take no more, so I shook my fist at him and ran to get a club to drive him out."

From this a lesson can be drawn that one must read the true meaning into silence. It shows how deceptive the mind can be if not quiet and under control. To the noble and serene silence is bliss, while to the impure and the disturbed silence is torture.

The silence need not be sad, dull, or under suspicion as it was to the one-eyed monk. Because you are silent in mind does not mean you are unhappy, melancholy, or averse to your fellowmen. Our minds and our emotional life are so accustomed to incessant activity that without it no interest in life and no joy in it seems possible. Life is insufferable, a disease of boredom, unless one is rushing here and there. But the spiritual is not found in this way.

The prophet Elijah says that it was not in the earthquake or the fire that he heard God but as a still, small voice.[7] It is in the silence of the soul that we listen for the Divine. As the Bible says, God comes quietly like a thief in the night, to enrich us with the treasures of his glory and the ecstacy of his joy. This is the silence beyond all utterance and thought, the peace that Paul said passes all understanding, the joy that Simon Peter said is unspeakable.

---

[7] I Kings 19:12.

CHAPTER VI

MYSTICAL EXPERIENCE

MYSTICAL EXPERIENCE

Mysticism has the aura of reality. There is no spectrum of life into which its hues and colors do not reach like the rainbow spans the earth. The tenor of all human activities reflects its potency and responds to its veiled touch. Let us consider, for example, Abraham Lincoln, of whom it has been said that the mystical in him showed up as clearly as the veins in a block of marble; he was a man of prophetic presentiments. The concluding sentences of his first inaugural address as President of the United States declared: "Though passion may have strained, it must not break our bonds of affection. The mystic chords of memory, stretching from every battlefield and every patriot grave to every living heart and hearthstone all over this broad land, will yet swell the chorus of the Union when again touched, as surely they will be, by the better angels of our nature."

The greatest statesmen of the race have always been those who, like Lincoln, where able to instill the overtones of the mystic into their orations, and thus to add to the rightness of their cause the magic power of poetry. It has been said that no great statesman ever lived who did not have this gift in his public utterances. It is the mark of the great orator.

Poetry itself lives and breathes in the mystical as its proper domain. Consider these verses:

> A primrose by the river's brim
> Only a primrose was to him.

In these lines the poet rebukes those who see in the flower only its physical beauty, lovely as that is. He directs us to an absolute beauty beyond, to a vista of charm, grace, measure, color and rhythm, which far exceed all beauty that physical senses and the mind can communicate.

In everyday life also, the individual has mystical intimations by which he feels that he sees beneath the surface of events and circumstances, and looks into the future. People have premonitions or receive intuitions that impel them to prefer one course of action above another, to do this and not that, to stay here or go there. They call this telepathy, extrasensory preception, or say they themselves are psychic. Often they say that they will "sleep on the matter." By this they mean that when the mental consciousness is quiet, and at rest during slumber, some truth from a deeper consciousness than the mind will suddenly solve a pressing problem and reveal to them, on awakening, the right thing to do.

Mysticism also deeply affects the collective life. As there is an individual psyche or soul, so there is the collective nation soul, and the world soul of man. The passage quoted from Lincoln demonstrates this. He appeals to the nation soul to preserve the union of a free people. He calls on the bond of affection, patriotism, and the mystic beings of the spirit — the better angels of our nature, as he expresses it — and says that surely these will rise higher than any human passion to save the Union. It was this mystic force exemplified in Lincoln which, more than anything else, was to turn the tide of Civil War, and save the United States from dissolution, which would have been a disaster, not only to our country, but to the cause of world freedom today.

Mysticism reaches its heights in spiritual experience. It is said that all individual religious experience rises from mystical planes of consciousness. All the world religions have embodied this in their teaching and inculcated it in their followers. Christians, Jews, Hindus, Buddhists and Moslems all have done this.

Christianity, especially in its earlier centuries, had many mystics and much mysticism. Mysticism was attained through what the Catholics called "orison," which means meditation. Definite disciplines and methods were utilized to raise the soul to oneness with God. In richness and variety some of the Catholic orisons are reminiscent of the yogic mediative practices of India, except for outer differences, such as posture.

The Catholics did not sit cross-legged, but they did adopt such things as manuals of spiritual exercises, step-by-step movement from one spiritual scene to another. By these methods they sought gradually to elevate the spiritual consciousnes until God or Christ came to posses the entire mentality.

That this practice of meditation to attain mystical experience is universal is not surprising. There has always been a spiritual interchange among races and nations. Even in the days of Christ and before, there was an interflow of spiritual knowledge and practices between East and West.

The Protestants, however, expecially the Evangelicals, divested themselves of the orison. This was part of the Protestant reaction against Catholicism. Meditation to the Protestant became a matter of earnest prayer, when need for it was felt, and not a system of spiritual devotions methodically arranged and regularly practiced. The word "orison" itself is unfamiliar to most Protestants.

It has only been in recent years that a number of the newly-founded and independent churches in this country have begun to restore intensive meditation to a more respected status. It has a regular place in their spiritual systems, if not in the fullness, regularity and scope that is enjoyed in Catholicism and has always possessed in the Orient.

Let us give a Catholic example: St. John of the Cross said that in orison the soul is in a union of love with God, reached by contemplation in which God pervades the soul. We receive, he says, this mystical knowledge of God in none of the kind of images, none of the sensible representations, which our mind makes use of in other circumstances . . . since the senses and the imagination are not employed, we get neither form nor impression, nor can we give any account or likeness, although the mysterious and sweet-tasting wisdom comes home so clearly to the inmost parts of our soul.

Now what are the practical effects of these mystical experiences upon the outer life of the mystic? Saint Ignatius was a mystic, but he became also one of the most dynamic, forceful and practical workers in the history of the Catholic Church. St. John of the Cross says that mystical experiences enrich life marvelously. He says, "A single meditation may be sufficient to abolish at a stroke certain imperfections of which the soul, during its entire life, had vainly tried to rid itself and to leave it adorned with virtues and supernatural gifts."

Saint Theresa described the results of orison or meditation in such words as these: "Often, infirm and wrought upon with dreadful pain, the soul emerges from it full of health and admirably disposed for action . . . as if God had willed that the body itself, already obedient to the soul's desires, should share in the soul's happiness."

One may be prompted to inquire as to why, in view of these sublime experiences and happy results, Protestants abandoned orison along with much else in Catholicism. Some of the reason is to be found in the kind of negative theology which also is included in the orisons, and which not even all Catholics could accept.

Thus, St. John of the Cross says that in meditation the soul is seized with a strange torment — that of not being allowed to suffer enough. Saint Theresa speaks of soaring desires, heroic resolutions, which are yet accompanied by horror of the world, and our own proper nothingness. It is gloomy, self-punishing doctrines such as these which have caused some noted theologians to declare that Christian theology is pessimistic, world-denying and life-negating.

The joy of the meditation was dampened by the gloom of the theology. Ecstasy of the spirit was pulled down by castigation of the world. It was as if God were loved and glorified as the Creator, but not for what He created. This is a metaphysical anomaly, and inherent contradiction, and against it reaction was inevitable. This pessimism cannot be laid at the door of Catholicism only, for it lingers on in Protestant theology also.

Catholics were on solid ground in holding to the practice of orison or meditation as such. Protestants and others were on an equally firm footing in rejecting it in part, because of the pessimistic theology it often contained. The remedy is not to throw away the meditation, but only the foreign mental admixtures of dogma which have gotten into it. You can meditate to spiritual gain without looking on the world as horror, and yourself as nothingness. Modern psychologists have commented on this; they have cautioned that to look on the world and yourself morbidly is not healthy-minded.

When you meditate on the Divine, you should be able to see the beauty and holiness of God beneath everything and under all disguises, as did the great Hasidic Rabbi, the Baal-Shem-Tov, who saw joy in everything and God everywhere. You will see yourself not as nothingness, but as a child of the Divine Being, perfected in the conditons of nature.

Let us refer briefly, now, to the mystical systems of the other world religions. The two principal ones of Indian origin are Hinduism and Buddhism. In Hinduism, the object of meditation is union with God. This system is a detailed spiritual discipline requiring special exercises, posture, diet, mental concentration and ethical purity. By these means the devotee, using what might be called a *scientific thoroughness of process,* attains ultimate union with God. This attainment is expressed in the Upanishads as crossing the boundry to the real self. When the real self is discovered, day and night cross not that boundary, nor old age nor death; neither grief nor pleasure, neither good nor evil deeds. All evil shuns the real self, which is free from impurity. When he has crossed that boundary, if he is blind, he sees; if he is wounded, he is healed; if he is afflicted, he ceases to be afflicted; for the world of Brahman is light itself. Such is the mystical experience of Hinduism.

The most familiar symbol of Buddhism is the image of Buddha seated in meditation. But both the system and the object differ from that of Hinduism. The Buddhist in meditation first concentrates the mind; next, the mind function ceases and unity remains; then the sense of unity goes, and indifference sets in; next, the devotee says that nothing exists. There are no ideas and no absence of ideas. He goes on until, in meditation, he comes as close as possible to annihilation, the void, the silence, immersion in the impersonal Buddhist Absolute. The Hindu finds God in meditation; the Buddhist finds the void.

In Mohammedanism, the mystics have been chiefly the Sufis, and the Dervishes. Let us quote briefly from a Persian Sufi, a philosopher and theologian of the Eleventh Century. He wrote that the end of Sufism is total absorption in God . . . from the beginning, revelations take place in so flagrant a shape that the Sufis see before them, while wide-awake, the angels and the souls of the Prophets; they hear their voices and obtain their favors. Then the transport rises from the perception of forms and figures to a degree which escapes all expression, and which no man may seek to give an account of without his words involving sin. So spoke the Sufis of mystical experience in meditation.

As to Judaism, it is needless to say more than that from it sprang not only the mysticism of the Old Testament prophets, but of Christ, Paul and early Judaic Christianity. An instance is Paul's statement in Corinthians that he would go on to visions and revelations of the Lord, that he was caught up into the Third Heaven, and heard things that cannot be told; that man is not permitted to utter,[1] as the Persian Sufi was to say ten centuries later.

The last great surge of Jewish mysticism occurred in the late 17th and early 18th Century. Known as *Hasidism,* it was founded by the famous rabbi whom I have mentioned, the Baal-Shem-Tov, who died in 1760. The Baal-Shem-Tov found joy and holiness in all things and God everyhwhere. Rise

---

[1] II Cor. 12:1-4.

early in the morning, he said, and seize joy with might, for you are sanctified and a new man, and like God, create the world in your own image. This rabbi found joy and not horror in the world. Modern remnants of Hasidism persist to this day, but devoid of their original mystical depth and ecstasy.

Now that we have reviewed some of the mystical experiences of the past, what should it be like now and in the future? The first thing that should be said is that you are not obliged to meditate at all to have mystical experience. People have attained spiritual reliization without meditation, although most find it helpful.There is no pre-conceived, foreordained, or cut-and-dried system. Some individuals can meditate for hours, others for only a short time, and still others not at all. It depends on the individual temperament and the spiritual path which that temperament inclines you to take. Whatever the path may be, if you aspire sincerely to the Divine, you will find the right way to meditate.

Do not think you are failing in your spiritual quest if you are not able to meditate like the Catholic saints, the Hindu yogis, or others. Some people virtually live in meditation; others, like Albert Schweitzer, say they have a mystical experience of God through the ethical performance of good deeds for others, whether in the jungles of equatorial Africa or elsewhere. Some approach God through philosophy or the intellect, and others through ardent love for the Divine. All of these paths meet and merge in an integral union with the Divine.

Methods for inducing meditation also vary widely. Some individuals begin by reading a passage of scripture; others keep before the inner eye an abstract or concrete image of God. Others begin by concentration of will in which all outer or phenomenal thoughts are excluded. The important thing, however, is to open yourself to the Divine Force, so It can descend into you constantly, posess you entirely, and express Itself in you completely. You will then feel the Divine Force settling in you, becoming more and more established. It will replace with Itself the lower motives of the nature which formerly held back your progress.

The test of true mystical experience is that it ceases to be mystical only, but also manifest in your natural instruments. All of your being — mind, emotions, body — will then be purified and transformed. Your life, like the existence of God, will be delight. You will experience the joy, strength, and healings which, as the saints have testified, flow into one during meditation. Difficulties and diseases which once vexed you will now yield. You will be able first to check, then to establish control over them, and finally to conquer them.

A higher light will open to you as a result of mystical experience. In counseling others I have often encountered earnestly religious people who were wrestling in their minds with some spiritual problem. With the best possible intentions they were, nevertheless, wrestling in the wrong place, or rather with the wrong kind of self-strength. Consequently they could not win the victory and find the answer until this was corrected.

In what way were they wrestling wrong? They were wrestling a spiritual or mystical problem with the mental faculty, and therefore could not prevail. You may pin the mental shoulders of an opponent to the mat in the ring of reason — but the Spirit is not ringed about with anything, including the ropes of the mind. You have to get out of that relatively small "ring" and into the vastness of million-fold realms of that Spirit if you are to discover Divine Truth.

"Which of you," asked Christ, "by taking thought can add a cubit to his stature?" In the same vein, Aurobindo, one of the foremost modern sages, said, "I never think; I either see or I don't see." One of the ancient Roman emperors had some Jewish rabbis brought before him to explain, in peril of their lives, why they refused to worship an image of the emperor as God.

The rabbis answered that the God they worshipped was All-Powerful, and could not be looked at by the human eye. The emperor asked, "How, then, do you know that your God exists, and is all-powerful?"

"Can you look at the noon-day sun with your naked eyes?" asked the rabbis. "No," replied the emperor. "Then," said the rabbis, "if you cannot look at the sun which God created, how can you look at God Who created not only the sun, but the heavens and the earth and all that is therein?"

Thus we cannot see the Divine Light through the senses and the mind; but we can discern it through the soul. When It descends into us, we receive the Holy Spirit, the Comforter that Christ said he would send when he was gone, even the Spirit of Truth that will reveal to us all things. This is not to belittle the mind, or the body either, for that matter. They are necessary, each in its place, for in the body we have our physical foundation; with the mind we think; but with the soul, we know, and enter the glorious presence of God.

These things we know to be true through our own individual spiritual or mystical experience. We know it, also, by the testimony of all the best and greatest among men, the very incarnations and prophets of the Divine, who have brought humanity the highest hopes, the largest good and the sweetest blessings. As Christ said to Nicodemus, "Verily, verily, I say unto thee, we speak that we know, and testify that we have seen, and ye receive not our witness. If I have told you earthly things and ye have not believed, how shall ye believe if I tell you of heavenly thngs? And no man has ascended up to heaven but he that came down from heaven, even the Son of Man, which is in heaven."[2]

---

[2]John 3:11-13.

CHAPTER VII

THE CONCRETE EFFECT
OF SPIRITUAL FORCE

THE CONCRETE EFFECT OF SPIRITUAL FORCE

Since remotest times man has observed and believed in the concrete effect of spiritual force on his life and that of the world. These forces to him have been more powerful and palpable than all others, exceeding by far those of man and Nature. He has sung and written of this faith in countless scriptures and in verses without number.

"Where were you," said the Lord to Job, "when I laid the foundations of the earth?" In the vast cosmos and the wheeling of the stars, in large and in small, in the seen and the unseen, man has felt the effect of spiritual force, guiding his actions toward a safe haven, and guarding him from danger and disaster. Yet, to be aware of this force is one thing. To make it fully concrete and effective in your life is quite another. We may be convinced that it exists, yet need guidance in applying it to our being and our activities. Three steps are necessary for this purpose: First, to realize that spiritual consciousness has force; Second, to realize that this force has concrete and tangible effectivity upon the being; and Third, to understand the ways in which the force makes Its consequences operative, or withholds them.

Let us consider these steps one by one, beginning with the first: The force of spiritual consciousness is an unseen energy. This should be hardly debatable. But there is nothing unreal about unseen forces. There are many other kinds of unseen forces in addition to invisible spiritual force. Among these are mental, psychological and physical forces that we cannot see. For example: The thought waves of others affect us. Often identical thoughts or words will spring up in the minds of two individuals without any other communication between them. People often say to each other, "I was thinking the same thing." This is called mental telepathy. Also, in the presence of a strong-minded person, others are often swayed and persuaded by the force of his thoughts.

The same is true of emotions. Angry people can inflame others by the unseen impact of their fury, whether they are present or absent. We react to the anger by becoming disturbed ourselves, or throwing off the other person's wrath. Similarly, a cheerful person can often change the atmosphere around others to one of optimism and geniality.

It is the very realm of the physical itself, however, that the power of unseen force is most obvious. Those who insist that only the physical is concrete, find on deeper scrutiny that here the unseen is emperor of all. Matter is affected by unseen cosmic rays, x-rays, electricity, atomic and sub-atomic energy, by the forces of gravitation and relativity.

As to spiritual force, there can be no such thing if it is not effective. A force is not a force if it cannot achieve results. What is God, and what is His power if it is not concretely effective? The fact that this force operates in ways that may not seem concrete and tangible to us does not matter. It is not an illusion because it is unseen, as we may surmise from the findings of science itself.

Science now knows that everything in the world is a form of energy. Religion had this understanding thousands of years before modern science demonstrated that it is mathematically provable under Einstein's equations. "In God," said the Apostle Paul, "we live, move, and have our being." According to the Vendanta of India, perhaps the world's most ancient sacred scriptures, all the world is said to be a play of a power of a spiritual entity, the power of an original consciousness.

In a speech to the National Academy of Sciences, Dr. I. I. Rabi, of Columbia University, a famous scientist and winner of the Nobel Prize, said: "The urge to comprehend the visible and invisible forces of the universe and to find man's place within it is common to both science and religion. In pursuing these aims," said Dr. Rabi, "religion has always taken the lead. It came first . . . it could not wait for the discovery of the neutron and the development of the theory of evolution . . . science, on the other hand, can never hope to deal in certitudes. Scientists are well aware that they are prone to error . . . for the scientist's nature is enigmatic, always miraculous in its originality . . . The scientist wants to broaden and deepen our knowledge and understanding of everything. But his work is no substitute for religious faith and certainty and finality. Scientific curiosity,'' said Rabi, ''will never be satisfied because it will never reach its goal, to know all and to understand all.'' As a spiritual teacher expressed it, ''There can be no action without force or energy doing the action and bringing about its consequences.'' Anything without force is either dead, inert, or unreal and without consciousness. Spiritual consciousness has no reality if it does not have effective force.

Let us pass now to the second step: The effectivity of spiritual force upon the being. There is the Divine Force which we call down from above. There is also the spiritual teacher or prophet, the divine representative. In him there, also, is both spiritual consciousness and force. Men are drawn to him by this inner power that he possesses. ''Follow me,'' said Christ to those whom he selected, and they left their nets and their tax collections to do as he commanded. spiritual force brings spiritual results.

There is also the force in the life of individuals generally. When an individual says that he feels it to be the direction of the spirit that he take a certain course of action, go here or there, do this or the other, it is not to be regarded as an illusion. This has happened to many people as they will attest, with the most auspicious results. It is not an illusion, but in some people it can be a delusion. Such people are deluded into mistaking the promptings of their lower nature for a divine command. But the spiritual force is not the less real because of any attempted misuse of its power.

The attempted misuse of power is not restricted to the spiritual. Is not political, economic, social, or military power often misused? Are there no misguided policies and false leaders that beckon to man in these activities? Christ warned of false prophets who would come in his name. ''Such men,'' said the Apostle Paul, ''are false prophets, deceitful workmen, disguising themselves as Apostles of Christ. And no wonder,'' says Paul, ''for even Satan disguises himself as an Angel of Light. So it is not strange if his servants also disguise themselves as servants of righteousness. Their end will correspond to their deeds . . . We cannot do anything against the truth but only for the truth.''

We turn now to the third and last step: How the spiritual force concretely funtions or withholds itself. How, for instance, does the force become effective in illness? Why are some people healed by spiritual force while others are not? Have you tried to heal yourself of illness by spiritual force and failed, and if so, why?

It is a fact that spiritual force has healed many people of disease. This may occur in a number of ways, any of which is admissible. The immediate agency may be a true spiritual teacher or guide from whom the healing power emanates. Even in medical practice, it has been said that some doctors do more to heal their patients through an inner force they possess than by the medicines they prescribe. It is for this reason that patients often prefer one doctor over another, because they feel in the one they choose some force that gives them strength and confidence and assurance of recovery.

There are many doctors who are consciously aware that it is the force of the Divine that is working to heal through the medicines they dispense and the operations they perform. Some patients get well with an amazing rapidity which medical science cannot explain. In such cases the patient can feel the spiritual force working in him and the doctor does not hesitate to credit it.

This does not mean that the spiritual force has what we call success in all instances. It is not arbitrary or unpredictable but works under the conditions of things. If there is no receptivity or assent in the indivdual to its working in him; if the indivdual does not surrender himself to the divine power, or if there is a hostile refusal even to admit that spiritual force can heal, certainly it will withdraw. This should not be hard to understand. Even your doctor will withdraw if you refuse his services. The force will not heal anyone by spiritual power who does not open to that power, or will heal only slowly or imperfectly if the opening is slow and not complete. Sometimes too much damage has been done to the physical structure before a call is at last made to the divine force. You can turn to God too late, just as you can get to the hospital too late.

God works under the conditions of the creation. That is why Christ refused to hurl himself from the pinnacle of the temple. He knew that if he did, he would be crushed to death on the stones of the courtyard below. The spiritual force would not have borne him up in such a foolish and needless act which would prove nothing and serve no useful purpose. Christ was not a magician. God did not send him to amaze people, but to be a witness of the Truth, the truth of Nature as well as the truth of the Spirit, both of which are different sides of the One Divine Truth-Reality.

You, as an individual, may attempt to influence another to lead the spiritual life. This is commendable but not enough to change the other person's nature if there is some pride, indolence, presumption, or doubt in his being. The change is possible only if his soul turns to the Divine. That responsibility rests with him. If there is rejection and hostility you are under no obligation to try further. That is why Christ said, "Do not cast your pearls before swine, lest they turn and rend you." The essence of the Divine is liberation, and God compels no one, but sanctions freedom of choice, as befits the spirit within you.

Spiritual force is not an enigma. It works under conditions and limits more scrupulously exact and inviolable than any by which science is governed. Can spiritual force override such conditions and limits? It can, but does so rarely. The Divine could have overridden the might of the Roman Empire and saved Christ from crucifixion. But men were not yet ready to receive the word he was teaching. Their ignorance rejected the truth he was speaking. As men in succeeding generations became more developed and open to that truth, he was taken from the cross of humiliation to be worshipped as an incarnation of God by the multitudes. The career and crucifixion of Christ became one of the main events of human history. Christ came that the Spirit should be in the conditions of life and not a force apart from it. That is why he said to Pilate, *If my kingdom were of this world, then would my servants fight . . . but now is my kingdom not from hence.* The conditions for that, Christ meant are not yet here. He meant that the kingdom is not now, but is to come; the spiritual force that is not wholly effective to men now will be all-effective to them then.[1]

The spiritual force exerts pressure to change conditions and remove the limits that restrain its effectivity. It can transform all of our instruments and faculties. It can enlarge the mind, add new fields of knowledge, acquire new capacities for us and expand old ones, uplift character and brings its influence to bear on men and things. It can control the processes of the body in a proper regulation and influence other forces.

The action of spiritual force is not vague, abstract, tenuous or weak. We can feel it massively, channel, direct and concentrate it wherever needed. We can observe its movements, be aware of its volume and dynamism, and how to use it to overcome unspiritual and hostile forces. In fatigue, its infinite strength can pour into us to restore energy; in illness, its purifying force and light can be intensely concentrated on the area or organ of the body that is diseased, re-shaping, checking any further deterioration, and healing. What we have said about fatigue and illness applies also to the correction of all other defects and weakneses in our being, for our transformation and perfection through concrete application of spiritual force. As we become more aware of the inner forces and strengthen our faith in them, we can "see, follow, and use their workings, just as the scientist uses the unseen forces of Nature."

---

[1]John 18:36.

The individual's actual experience of the spiritual force will finally become customary, daily, and normal to him. He himself will become an effective force of this Divine Force. None of this is possible by any method, however, if we allow the mind to raise the spectre of doubt. "I can doubt all things if, in the end, it leads me," in the words of Paul, "to believe all things." But doubt for doubt's sake, that refuses to seek or believe anything, is a useless and empty creed. No scientist could ever succeed if he proceeded in this way. If he doubts a certain axiom it is because he thinks that a better one can be predicated. What is the physical mind itself that it can question spiritual force? How does the mind know that it exists and works? If it is conscious, what makes it conscious?

In all walks of life it is not the doubter to whom man looks as a guide. It is those who direct men to search for and believe in deep principles, unseen universal forces, cosmic influences, and divine truths who are a light to the world. Such men perceive the underlying meaning and direction of things, and the course that individuals and society should take for their liberation, peace and happiness.

No prophet, statesman, warrior, or scientist whose life and deeds have benefited mankind has ever doubted the truths which he revealed, or for which he struggled, or which he put to use for the good of the human race. "God is a Spirit and the Truth," says the Bible, "yet He made the heavens and the earth and all that is therein."

The Apostle Paul reminded the Colossians that the spirit in his words, "is the head of all rule and authority . . . I say this that no one may delude you with beguiling speech . . . See that no one makes a prey of you by philosophy and empty deceit, according to human traditions and not according to Christ."

Let us not be of those of whom Paul said, "A veil lies over their minds, but when a man turns to the Lord the veil is removed. Now the Lord is the Spirit, and where the Spirit of the Lord is, there is freedom. And we all, with unveiled faces, beholding the glory of the Lord, are being changed into his likeness from one degree of glory to another; for this comes from the Lord who is the Spirit."[2]

---

[2] II Cor. 3:15-18.

CHAPTER VIII

THE SPIRITUAL AND THE ETHICAL

THE SPIRITUAL AND THE ETHICAL

Clear distinction is not always made as to what constitutes the spiritual on the one hand and the ethical on the other. Many people deem them to be either equivalents or of like nature.

This impression receives support from the fact that every religion has an ethical or moral code as one of its salient features. Even the learned often have difficulty in perceiving the different nature and distinct capacity of the spiritual and the ethical. The line of demarcation between the metaphysical and the moral is not so easily discerned as some might think.

The tendency is to throw or shade them together as the same thing; or ethics is made paramount and the spiritual is consigned to the past as less suitable to the mentalized and scientific era of the present. The result is that men often single out or compile an ethical code from one or more of the moral codes of the great world religions. Either consciously or unconsciously they substitute this for the spiritual. Whenever the subject rises, they are prone to say, "Follow the Golden Rule," or to cite some other sound and accepted religious ethical teaching, and to consider that this is all that man need know or say regarding the spiritual, the Infinite and Eternal.

Now such people are often admirable individuals and good citizens in many ways. Some of them become social, political or cultural reformers. They are frequently fired with the ideal that by devotion to their ethics they can attain spiritual progress. In many cases they devote themselves with considerable personal sacrifice to humanitarian deeds rendered under difficult circumstances, or to those in far-off or backward parts of the world.

This is something tangible, practical, and rationally understandable to the ethicists. To love your neighbor, to be humble and charitable are precepts which they grasp easily with the mind. To carry out these precepts by helpful deeds is to translate them into action, the results of which they can see. But they are less at home and frequently not at ease in the spiritual, the mystical, the divine; that is beyond the perception of the senses and the limits of the human mind.

In some respects, mankind in a more remote and earlier day had a better understanding of the distinction between the spiritual and the ethical, and of the relationship between the spiritual and the ethical, than does the predominantly rational person, the empirical scientific individual of today. An example is the Ten Commandments, which are primarily an ethical code. Yet the scriptures declare that these injunctions were handed down from God to man. They were of spiritual origin and purpose; they came from the Divine to lead men to the Divine. They were not an ethical code devised by man to lead him to certain elevated moral goals. even though those goals are good and necessary in themselves.

There is a reason for the frequent failure to discern the difference between the spiritual and the ethical. It is because of the tendency of present human consciousness to confine itself to physical reality. In most cases, we want a rule or ethical law to guide us as to what to do. We are less concerned with the supraphysical, the immense imponderable of the Divine. As a result, human egoism is apt to imprison us in the narrow closure of materiality. It inclines us to shrink from any exursions of our being into the vast, the infinite. In this way, we close off our deeper comprehensions and our profounder insights. This reduces man from supremacy over nature to subserviency to it.

Christ encountered some of his severest opposition due to human inability to discern this difference between the spiritual and the ethical. He came to preach a great new spiritual revelation. Yet in the constricted minds of his opposition there arose only accusations against him; such as plucking corn on the Sabbath, contrary to the moral law of the Hebrews of that time. Christ on other occasions modified the moral law. He saved the life of the adultress. The extreme punishment of death for that offense under the moral law of that time would not be meted out under the ethical laws of today. Thus, as one author has said, Man in his ignorance "regards the social and moral laws of his time as something absolute and immutable; as a matter of fact, they are temporal and conventional, and they cannot serve as a guide in the deeper crises of life.''[1]

The history of man's evolution also proves that it is the spiritual which gives rise to the ethical. We have already cited the instance of the Ten Commandments. Primitive man was always religious. Remnants of primitive society still in existence in isolated parts of the world, and archeological evidence, substantiate this beyond any doubt. Man's first religion was an awareness of a higher force or higher presence above and about him. That force or presence, he believed, would respond to his needs and to his pleas for aid and healing, if only he could please and propitiate those forces and avoid their wrath and merit their favor.

Out of this there arose a frequently superstitious or mysterious cult of rituals, sacrifices, and magic. There were no moral codes as such. But as man's ego and mentality developed, the spiritual within us brought a demand for an ethical regulation of his life. It was a psychic call to render our activities responsive to the expanding light within him. This was reflected in the ethical codes of the various religions. Man has reached an enlarged preception, a comprehension of paths by which he could attain a harmonious and peaceful society. These paths were laid before man in revelations such as the Decalogue of Moses and the Sermon on the Mount of Christ.

The author, Rischabhchand, says that sociologists claim that morality results from increasing social pressure. Their theory is that an ethical discipline and regulation of life is required to encounter the menace of disruptive and antisocial tendencies.[2] Morality, according to them, is ''a material growth, a covenant and convenience agreed upon for the smooth running of the wheels of life.'' To them the source of morality is social and not spiritual. But the well-springs of ethics are not in the outer mechanism of the individual or the collective existence. It stems from two inner things.

The first is the evolutionary development of human reason. The second is the balancing and enlightening principle of poise, knowledge, and the satisfaction of the innate and eternal power of existence in man. Ethics is, therefore, a spiritual gift. It is the product of a contact of the human consciousness with a Higher Consciousness.[3]

---

[1] Anilbaran Roy, *The Gita* (Pondicherry: Sri Aurobindo Ashram Press, 1954) p. 13.

[2] Rischabhchand, *In the Mother's Light* (Pondicherry: Sri Aurobindo Ashram Press, 1954) p. 13.

[3] Rischabhchand, *In the Mother's Light* (Pondicherry: Sri Aurobindo Ashram Press, 1954) p. 13.

The ethical codes and laws of the religions are ancient and exalted. Yet their strictures have not become the entire ruler of life as the religions would be the first to concede. They have acted as a restraining and ennobling influence for which all should be thankful. Yet at the same time the world is still a scene of many actions which are not ethical, much less spiritual. Why is this? Man believes in his ethical codes and moral laws. Why, then, has he not been more successful in following them? Why is it that they have accomplished so much, yet failed in so much?

When ethical codes are formulated in society, they tend to be compromised or diluted in such a way as to lose much of their potential for control and regulation of life. There are several causes for this. Ethics may become a form of mental prohibition. It may become merely a repressive force which spiritually, psychologically and socially is unable to cope with the "obstinate concerted" elements of man's lower nature. The Old Adam in man refuses to listen. Observance of ethical codes may become superficial or a pretense, or may honor but overlook major offenses against the heart of its standards.

Morality may go to rude extremes. It may adopt harsh, bare, self-mortifying, even cruel measures. It may insist on a rigid sameness that is inconsistent with freedom of the spirit.

It can also be adulterated to a narrow ethicism which is dismal, gloomy, and corrosively and morbidly Puritanical. In this vein it may frown upon or reject music, art, and other beauties and comforts of gracious living as sinful or outlawed. This attitude forgets that the spiritual includes not only the pure and the ethical, but also love, joy, mercy, gentleness, compassion, a sweet gaiety of the soul, and all the marvelous variety, yet oneness, of the Infinite.

As has already been said, none of this should keep us from recognizing the great and indispensable contributions of ethics to human culture, but useful as these have been, man must exceed these achievements and go beyond their inherent limitations. Just as man arose from primitive cults to ethical consciousness, he must rise yet higher to spiritual consciousness. The moralist should travel on from his mind-constructed ethics to a higher plane. He should not stop at the half-way house of ethics, even if it is a well-ordered and harmonious habitation. Ethics is only a phase, even if a very high one, in the ascent of human consciousness. If man stops there, he incurs two disadvantages: First, if past experience is any guide, his ethical codes alone will not bring to him and the world the peace and happiness that he seeks. Second, he loses the power and privilege of his ultimate fulfillment.

Deliverance for man is in his sincere aspiration and self-surrender to a higher light, to the native light and force of the spirit . . . this is at once the sole means and the end of man's self-transcendance . . . a genuine spiritual experience is not like a mental thought, idea or imagination. It comes from the unexplored depths or heights of the being and leaves an indelible impression on the consciousness, or gives it at once a new and decisive orientation. It is the only power that can lift man out of the morass of his ordinary existence. It is the only power that can awaken his soul and make it the master of his nature.[4]

Neither prescribed and rigid ethical codes nor fixed and unchangeable dogmas of religion can of themselves change or deliver society. They have attempted to do so thousands of years without success, even though they have been man's chief beneficial influence during all that time. It is the descent of the Spirit into man and society like a flash of lightning that "has to be infused into them to quicken a new birth." The Spirit is the essential truth of existence, and until that Spirit is manifested in the mind, life and body of the individual and in the material world, the maladies which vex humanity today in a seemingly endless stream will not be abated or healed. It is not through a mentalized ethical code or mental religious dogma that this will be achieved. It will be through a descent of the Spirit, such as fell upon the disciples of Christ at Pentecost, as with tongues of fire, and filled them with divine joy.

Man hesitates to take this leap into the spiritual, or to open himself to the divine power. It seems to us so immense, impalpable and undefined. How, we ask, can it descend into me? But there is no ingrained and insuperable obstacle or fault in people which condemns us to a life of half-intelligence and half-ignorance, half-order and half-disorder, such as we see about us today in the world. We are not destined to be forever partly in darkness and partly in light.

It is not intellect but egoism which holds us back. The ego in its pride and vanity leads us into arrogance, into an unwillingness to surrender to the Divine; but it is this very surrender, the flinging of ourselves into the spiritual, that is the next forward step in the evolution of man "if mankind is to transcend itself, not only in rare individuals, but as a race, and justify its existence on earth by a divine self-perfection."[5] Christ did not ask to be a

[4]Rischabhchand, *In the Mother's Light* (Pondicherry: Sri Aurobindo Ashram Press, 1954) pp. 90-91.

[5]Rischabhchand, *In the Mother's Light* (Pondicherry: Sri Aurobindo Ashram Press, 1954) p. 93.

rare individual or the only one that could do as he did. Christ said, "He who believes in me will do the works that I do; and greater works than these will he do."[6] This in a sense is the greatest prophecy of Christ for the future of the race.

Aurobindo said, "Therefore the individuals who will most help the future of humanity will be those who recognize spiritual evolution as the destiny and, therefore, the great need of the human being . . . they will be comparatively indifferent to particular belief and form and leave men to resort to the beliefs and forms to which they are naturally drawn. They will only hold as essential the faith in this spiritual conversion, the attempt to live it out and whatever knowledge — the form of opinion into which it is thrown — does not so much matter. They will especially not make the mistake of thinking that this change can be effected by machinery and outer institutions; they will know and never forget that it has to be lived out by each man inwardly, or it can never be made a reality for the kind."[7]

This does not mean that we should be indifferent to or neglect improvements in outer institutions required for the good of man and his society. It signifies that the perfection of existence will transpire through the embodiment of the spiritual in our lives.

Christ himself told the Parable of the Laborers. He said that the Kingdom of Heaven was like the householder who went out early in the morning to hire laborers for his vineyard. He agreed with them on a wage of a shilling for the day. Others he hired later in the day and yet later still others; but at the end of the work day, he paid them all the same wage.

Those who worked longest protested saying they had borne the burden and heat of the day, while some others had worked only an hour; yet all were paid the same. But the good householder answered: "I have done you no wrong; I paid you what I agreed. Take what is thine and go thy way; I will give unto this last even as unto thee. Is it not lawful for me to do what I will with mine own? Is thine eye evil because I am good? So the last shall be first and the first last; for many shall be called, but few chosen."[8]

Christ knew even if it happened that some men were located for the work later in the day and did not work as long as those who were found and

---

[6] St. John 14:12.

[7] Sri Aurobindo, *The Human Cycle*, Ch. 24.

[8] St. Matthew 20:1-6.

put to work earlier, nevertheless each man had the same need of money for that day's livelihood for himself and his family. So the good householder paid them all alike. From teachings such as this by Christ has arisen what is called the *Christian ethic*. This ethic has wrought in the Western world a remarkable advance in social conditions beyond anything previously known, and which the Eastern world is now trying to emulate. In the United States it has resulted in a concerted effort to remove the last vestiges of poverty from the nation, and France has proposed the yet broader object of obliterating poverty in the entire world.

Today religions support such causes as Civil Rights, the elimination of poverty in the nation and the world, a decent standard of living for all, human unity and world peace. Thus the record, ancient and modern, is that religion has always been a participant in the ethical improvement of human conditions, directly and indirectly, individually and socially.

There are those in the world today who call themselves workers for the betterment of human, economic and social conditions, and who at the same time deny that there is any spiritual life or that God exists. Pope Paul addressed himself to such atheists in his Easter message, 1964. He said, "Perhaps your idea of faith is erroneous, that it offends against intelligence, shackles progress, humiliates man, brings sadness to his life."

Let us say apropos the Pope's remarks, that spirituality does none of these things. Spirituality expands intelligence, unbinds the fetters of progress, takes the thorny crown of humiliation and mockery from the brow of man and instills joy in our life.

Without ethics, our society cannot become one where justice is not violated; without the spiritual it cannot become the Kingdom of God on earth in the new age of peace, light and joy.

The greater climax of the ethical is in a high purity of intelligence and will, an equability in the soul, a profound peace and calm, a universal sympathy and preparation of oneness. There will be a reflection of the soul's divine joy in mind, life and body. At this stage the ethical is already passing into the spiritual type and character. This culmination itself can be transcended, raised into a higher and freer light. It can pass into the settled God-like energy of the divine nature. There will then remain in us the Spirit's immaculate will and luminous force in all our members, acting in a wide and immovable calm and a deep and pure spiritual joy.[9]

---

[9] Anilbaran Roy, *The Gita* (Pondicherry: Sri Aurobindo Ashram Press, 1954) p. 263.

The New Consciousness

As the Apostle Paul wrote in his letter to the Romans, "For no human being will be justified in his sight by works of the law since through the law comes knowledge of sin. But now the righteousness of God has been manifested apart from law, although the law and the prophets bear witness to it, the righteousness of God through faith in Christ for all who believe . . . do we then overthrow the law by this faith? By no means! On the contrary, we uphold the law," said Paul.[10]

Such is the faith and the liberation taught by Christ. For as Christ said, "I tell you, something greater than the temple is here."[11]

---

[10] Romans 3:20-22, 31.
[11] St. Matthew 12:6.

CHAPTER IX

THE SPIRITUAL AND THE SOCIAL

THE SPIRITUAL AND THE SOCIAL

The relationship between the spiritual and the social has had a fundamental influence on the drift and the destiny of man's civilizations and cultures. It has had a determining effect as to whether they shall rise and flourish or decline and fall. In the course of history the spiritual and the social have sometimes been combined and at other times separate, sometimes in harmony and at other times put by man into needless opposition to each other.

Thus the functions of prophet and political military leader were combined in the cases of Moses and Mohammed, who exercised all authority, both spiritual and social, over their people, the Hebrews and the Arabs, respectively. Both Christ and Buddha, on the other hand, were spiritual leaders only; neither in his ministry held any political position or exercised any authority in the name of the state. Every generation, our own not excepted, has had to settle this issue between the spriitual and the eternal on one hand, and the worldly and the temporal on the other. It is the issue which underlies all other critical issues of the present era.

Let us, therefore, trace this relationship from its origins in the past to the modern era. Adequate past examples can be drawn from ancient cultures of Israel and India. In Biblical Israel in the case of Moses, all authority — spiritual, military and social — rested in him. The same was true with the prophet-judges who followed him. The last of these great judges was the prophet Samuel. But the Hebrew people demanded of Samuel that the two powers be separated. They called on him to anoint a human king to lead them in battle against the Phillistines, who were threatening their very existence. Samuel was reluctant to do this, but God said to Samuel, "Hearken to the voice of the people in all that they say to you; for they have not rejected you, but they have rejected me from being king over them."[1]

Samuel acceded, but not before he warned the Hebrews, in one of the superb passages of the Old Testament, of what a human king would be like. "He will make you run before his chariots," said Samuel; "he will take the best of your fields and orchards and give them to his servants, you shall pay heavy taxes and your sons and daughters shall labor for him; and you shall be his slaves."[2]

Having uttered this warning, Samuel gave in and annointed Saul, and later David, to be King over Israel. The monarchy was established and the line of kings whose reigns are recorded in the Books of Kings and Chronicles in the Bible. It was from the Davidic royal line that Christ descended.

Samuel did the only practical thing at this time to prevent the destruction of the Hebrews under existing circumstances. A central government had to replace the loose confederation of the twelve tribes for defense and other communal purposes. National, rather than tribal, organization had evolved and become inevitable.

The glories of this human kingdom did not last many centuries. It had succumbed to military conquest by the time Christ lived. Christ taught that the true kingdom — the Kingdom of God on earth — was now at hand, at the very gates. Men would no longer be the mortal slaves of a human ruler but the free and immortal sons of God in a divine age on earth.

In India many thousands of years ago, this question was settled by a strict caste system. At the top was the priestly or spiritual caste, known as the Brahmins. Second, came the warriors and rulers; third, merchants and traders; and fourth or last, the workers. In ancient India this arrangement had practical uses conforming to the natural proclivities of men. It did not prevent overlapping. Buddha, India's foremost spiritual teacher of antiquity, himself was not from the priestly, but the king, or warrior caste.

Buddha himself spoke against the caste system, saying that it is not

[1] I Samuel 8:3
[2] I Samuel 8:11-17

74

who one's mother or father is that determines whether a person is holy, enlightened, free from sin. The modern Hindu caste system has degenerated into an abusive, complex and rigid system which is a drag on India to this day. It is contrary to its original practical purposes in which the spiritual is placed at the summit of man's existence.

The Hindu caste system ultimately failed, as all such pruely external and doctrinal methods inevitably do. Oneness with God is attained only by the soul, not by caste, race, or creed.

Having reviewed these instances from the distant past, let us now turn to Europe of a thousand years ago, in the Christian Era. In the year 800 Pope Leo III crowned the King of the Franks, Charlemagne, as Emperor of the Holy Roman Empire. This was an alliance between the spiritual and the secular powers in which the Pope exercised a large and sometimes dominant influence, but the combination would not hold. The Pope and later emperors came into conflict. Historians have made the famous comment that the Empire was neither Holy nor Roman. After a few centuries the empire declined and was extinguished. Following the Reformation in Europe and the rise of Protestantism, the breach became final. Complete separation of church and state is the rule today in most Western nations, including our own.

The problem, nevertheless, still smolders in current controversies of our times. One of them was the issue that appeared before Congress and the country as to whether prayers or Bible-reading could be held in public schools, which are an arm of government. The Supreme Court has held this unconstitutional, as breaching the wall that divides church and state.

Another is the instance that occured in California a few years ago, when a Catholic priest asked the Pope to remove a Cardinal from office because the Cardinal held civil rights for minority races to be a political and not a moral question. The priest and his supporters held that the issue is both political and moral. The Cardinal sought to leave the civil rights issue to social province. The priest sought to bring it into the spiritual province as well. The priest is not alone in his position. Most of the religious leaders of the nation, including those of his own church, have taken like positions.

Thus fact, history, and contemporary happenings reveal that there are two diverse positions in this matter. One is that the spiritual or religious should not participate or meddle at all in social matters. The other is the opposite view that it should participate, the only question being as to how it can be most effective.

Let us first consider the negative, the non-participatory philosophy that separates religion and the world. In various theologies this appears as negative dogmas concerning the natural world and man who inhabits it. The world is held to be "a passing episode" or an illusion, a scene of evil and a veil of tears and sorrow. Man is held to be fallen and sinful by nature, and his only salvation an escape to the paradise or nirvana of another world. As eminent theologians have remarked, this tendency has made both Christian and Buddhist theologies pessimistic, world-denying and life-negating. Their gloomy world outlook is not to be found in Christ himself, but it nevertheless has become a familiar and potent force in Christian theology.

What is the practical effect of this attitude? How has society been affected by this negativism? It causes some ministers to deny that ideal conditions can ever occur on earth for the human race, and to discount the belief that man and world are perfectible. They declare that the perfected society, the divine age, Isaiah's prophecy that nations will learn war no more, Christ's Kingdom of God on earth, is all an unrealizable utopia.

The result, as was to be expected, has been a pessimistic social coloration which either withdraws from the world or manifests itself in retrogressive political, social, and economic theories, or sometimes in a mixture of both. As Christ said, "They do not enter themselves and do their utmost to prevent others from entering."[3] This position is socially unrealistic and religiously contrary to the teachings of Christ. Christ described the holders of this attitude in these words: "They lay heavy burdens on men and will not lift one finger to help them."

Let us turn now to the affirmative view which favors participation. The underlying principle of this world view is that the Divine is both transcendent and immanent, that is, both beyond and in nature and within men. Therefore, men and society are perfectible.

How should the spiritual exercise its force and mandate in the social? One approach calls for direct external intervention in world matters; the other relies chiefly on inner spiritual force.

First, let us consider the direct intervention. I have already given some examples of this, such as the strong stand of the clergy in this country for new civil rights laws. They also have pressed for many other social ameliorations, to end poverty, illiteracy and disease, etc. These are sufficient illustrations.

[3]Luke 11:52.

The other position holds that ministers should be spiritual teachers and not social workers. Christ was not a social worker, an office-holder, or a military captain, He came, as he told Pontius Pilate, to be a witness to the truth.

The invisible inner action of the spiritual force is more effective, concrete and dynamic than any outer force. This does not mean that the external sphere of works is to be neglected. The inner spiritual work is a source and a preparation for achieving the right external works more rapidly and on a firm and secure basis.

The external life is to be developed to its largest, widest, and best extent, both individually and in the social sphere. But this can fully occur only as the expression of inner spiritual realization. "The Kingdom of God without can be founded securely only on the Kingdom of God within." The inner spiritual force is not something metaphysical alone. To the contrary, it is the effective action of a supra-physical force, which is far more tangible and concrete in its physical effects than any force which science has at its command, or can devise.

The power of this inner force over outer events is illustrated in both the Old and the New Testaments. During the Exodus, the Hebrews met their first military resistance when the Amalekites attacked them near Mt. Sinai. The scriptures relate that so long as Moses held up his arms in prayer to God, the Hebrews prevailed, and through this means they won the battle. Invisible inner force gained the victory over the visible military power of the enemy.

In the New Testament there is the story of the centurion who asked Christ to heal his paralyzed servant who was in terrible distress. When Christ said, "I will come and heal him," the centurion replied that it would not be necessary. If only Christ would say the word, the servant would be healed. "I am a man under authority with soldiers under me," said the centurion, "and I say to one, 'Go,' and he goes, and to another 'Come,' and he comes." Thus did the centurion make the striking analogy that Christ, who was not under military authority, but spiritual authority, could send his unseen spiritual forces to heal the servant and it would be done. When Christ heard this he marveled and said that not even in Israel had he found faith like that of this Roman centurion. Christ said, "Go; be it done for you as you have believed," and the servant was healed at the very moment.[4]

[4]Mat. 8: 5-13.

The pessimistic theological outlook upon the world is losing ground today and most churches are more or less socially active. At the same time, the negative outlook, inculcated over so many centuries in human consciousness, continues to exercise a still strong, if waning, influence in social matters. It persists because the thought patterns of older theologies tend to stick in men's minds, even though the theology itself has risen from the foundations of the old to a new and broader faith.

The old habitual thought patterns are harder to dislodge than they were to entrench. Thus a theology which for many centuries has taught pessimism and prejudice concerning men and the world, when it wants to reverse itself and teach optimism and equality, finds it no easy task. An example is anti-Semitism. Organized Christianity for many centuries taught animosity against the Jews. Now Christianity deplores it and seeks to eradicate it. Yet the animosity sank deep into Western consciousness during past eras. Its roots are hard to get out, and anti-Semitic expressions unfortunately are still all too common.

It should be noted in passing that atheism, since it denies that the spiritual exists, also excludes the spiritual from paticipation in the social aspect of existence. Nevertheless, the change is in process and inevitable. Pessimism and negativeness will pass from social beliefs, as it is beginning to pass from theological doctrines.

Pope Paul VI declared that reaction against religion would occur if it opposes outer measures necessary for the social well-being of man. He said in an address in Rome, to an audience of the Congress of Christian Industrialists and Business Managers, "There must be something deeply wrong, radically insufficient, in the system itself if it originates such social reactions."

Thus did the Pope, like many other religious leaders, take the affirmative position of social concern. The spiritual and the social are two aspects of the one divine existence. The inner spiritual force is a growth of the soul into the dynamics of its full expression in outer life. Therefore, we should all labor to grow in the power of our inner work, so that its force will be felt in the world like that of God Whose invisible power shapes visible events for divine purpose. All will then transpire that is needful for the triumph of good and justice, and the defeat of evil and wrong in the world.

This is the true gospel in which we should labor. As the New Testament relates, "Christ went about all the cities and villages teaching in their synagogues and preaching the gospel of the Kingdom, and healing every disease and infirmity. When he saw the crowds, he had compassion for them because they were harrased and helpless, like sheep without a shepherd. Then he said to his disciples: ''The harvest is plentiful, but the laborers are few; pray therefore the Lord of the harvest that he may send out laborers into his harvest.''[5]

[5] Matt. 9:35-38.

CHAPTER X

DIVINE LOVE AND HUMAN LOVE

DIVINE LOVE AND HUMAN LOVE

Mankind deems love to be the loftiest sentiment of the human heart. As divine love it is the adoration of man for God and God for man; as human love it is affection for other human beings, for creatures and things in the natural world. Religion recognizes this distinction between divine love and human love. Christ said the First Commandment is to love God, and that the Second is like unto it: "Love thy neighbor as thyself." By this he meant that divine love is the highest, and human love is the second, a likeness, a reflection of divine love.

This distinction is found also in other religions. For example, Buddha said that the marriage bond is the happiest known to mortal man, but that husband and wife and all others should also be married to the Truth, which is immortal. The marriage to the Truth, Buddha said, endures forever.

Human love, happy as it is, has its frailties and impermanences. Sometimes it becomes but a shadow of its former self. Jealousy and inconsideration may cloud marriage or friendship. Love between parents and children is sometimes impared or lost. One religion remarks that parents sometimes raise children who turn out to be their enemies. Children may have grievances, real or imaginary, it matters not — against their parents. Some psychologists believe that children in given circumstances may have a secret subconscious hate for their parents which is the cause of nervous disorder in the child, which continues into adult life.

The science of psychology complements the spiritual. Psychology deals with mental processes; metaphysics or the spiritual deals with origin, meaning, and purpose of things, including the mind itself. It is not a derogation of the science of psychology or of any other science to say that no science can ever be a substitute for the certitude and salvation of the spiritual. With this the most eminent scientists agree.

The supreme aim of the spiritual quest is to bring divine love, beauty and joy into the world. Divine love descends in truth and power as something transcendental and universal that imparts itself to persons according to the divine will and purpose. It creates in us a greater and purer personal love than any which the human heart can now imagine. When you have felt this you can be an instrument for the advent and action of Divine love in the world.[1] Nothing else will fully stem the torrents of hate in the individual and in society that now too much disturbs our human existence.

The love that humans feel for each other is compounded of emotions, passion and desire. Emotion is excellent and necessary in human nature. Yet it has its perils. The emotions can get out of hand. They can overthrow equanimity and injure the life. They can deteriorate into lower impulses, or become intemperate, violent or revengeful.

This is true not only of human love but of other human faculties. The human mind is as excellent and indispensable in human nature as emotion is; but mind, like emotion, can also get out of hand. The thoughts can lead us not only in the paths of reason but sometimes contrary to reason and good sense. Man often has undeveloped or partly developed ideas. Who can look about us and say that man through his present ideas has become able to live perfectly? Does the state of the world warrant any such conclusion? Man is seeking to remedy this by going beyond present human mentality. We seek a higher mentality. We seek supra-mental knowledge free of the limitation and errors of the present human mind. That is why the Apostle Paul said that the thoughts of the wise are futile to the Lord. Man stands farther up the ladder of evolution than any other because of the rise in his consciousness and knowledge. Yet this must now be exceeded. In the same way that man is seeking to rise above the present human mind, he is likewise seeking to go beyond emotion to the height and depths and intensity of divine love. Just as his aim is to rise from mind to supermind, he aims to rise from human love to divine love. There he will feel in his psychic heart a perpetual oneness with

---

[1] *Letters of Sri Aurobindo,* First Series (Pondicherry: Sri Aurobindo Ashram Press, 1947) p. 231.

the Divine above and within all other beings, creatures and things.[2] How necessary it is to exceed human emotion and its lapses may be seen in our recent national crisis when from all quarters the cry has arisen for an end to hate, intemperate and extreme feelings.

Human love is subject to ego and desire. It often continues only so long as its cravings and demands are satisfied. If it does not get what it craves, or imagines it is not being treated as it should be, it will sulk, or turn from love to grief, hurt feelings, or anger. It may become a complex of imaginations misunderstandings, jealousies and misinterpretations. These can pyramid and multiply within until they crowd out whatever love remains; then there is only a pretense which is hard to maintain for beneath is resignation or bitterness.

Such provides no true basis for human love and certainly none for divine love. All such feelings in human love should be eliminated. Love should be a crown of joy and union, mutual faith, and self-giving. The lower ways of human love result only in pain, trouble, dissatisfaction, disillusion, disunion. Even the slightest amount of this poison should not be tolerated. It has a deadly effect.[3] One word or glance of it is enough to spoil our day. Such are the ills that human love is often heir to.

Human love at its best approaches Divine love. Divine love is not jealous, possessive, monopolistic, or demanding. Love for God is self-surrendering, demands nothing, does not stipulate conditions or drive bargains. The disturbances of wounded vanity, bruised pride, and resentful anger are absent from divine love.

Pure human love is altogether self-giving. "Greater love hath no man," said Christ, "than that he lay down his life for his friend." But the love of God for man in return for man's love is the greatest of all self-givings, for God gives Himself to his devotees in entirety and freedom. The divine love takes charge of all planes of your being; it refashions and guides all of them to perfection and raises you in the divine arms to God.

Divine love is greater and more enduring than human love. This is because it is the soul in us that is eternal and endures. Therefore, only that love which has its source in the soul is greatest and eternal.

[3] *Letters of Sri Aurobindo*, First Series (Pondicherry: Sri Aurobindo Ashram Press, 1947) p. 325.
[2] *Letters of Sri Aurobindo*, First Series (Pondicherry: Sri Aurobindo Ashram Press, 1947) p. 232.

The fire of divine love is warm, intense and radiant. It is pure and burns without the smoke of desire or the ashes of grief. As a philosopher has said, divine love is personal but not egoistic; it goes from the real being in the one to the real being in the other. For that, liberation from the ordinary human approach is necessary.

Divine love is universal, all-inclusive, yet personal and individual. It loves all alike, yet its love is especially felt by the individual. It is general, yet particular, impersonal yet personal.

Whoever loves particular individuals only, but not mankind, does not possess divine love. Likewise, those who profess an abstract love for mankind, but cannot feel a warm personal love for the individual, do not possess divine love. As John says in the Bible, "He who says that he loves God and does not love man is a liar."

Divine love has warmth and bliss, yet is tranquil. The vision of the divine countenance awakes in us a glow of adoration accompanied by an immense, indescribable calm and peace that lightens the body as if it were pure spirit. Human love is sometimes unrequited, but divine love never. It is as if God were powerless to resist the proffer of devotion to Him, as if He abdicates His very supremacy to answer the call of adoration that rises to Him. "I will not be late to answer," He seems to say. "I will not let you be tried beyond your strength, and my angels will bear you up, lest you dash your foot against a stone."

To love divinely, one must become divine in nature. This requires transformation of the nature, the re-birth of which Christ spoke. Unless you become a new and higher creature, you cannot have this new and higher love. Man in his evolution has risen from animalistic love to human love, and is to rise from human love to divine love. It is as inevitable that man will rise from human to divine love as it was that he arose from animalistic love to human love. He was not fixed at the animal level, nor will he remain at the present human level.

Human love is not only subject to disillusionment and disaffection between individuals, but between groups. Estrangement among groups or class lines is now frequent. This occurs not only within but between countries. Nations may be allies at one moment and enemies the next. They may fight side by side in one war, and when it is over their enemies often become their allies, and their one-time allies become their enemies in preparation for the next war.

Nations are in the divorce court as frequently as individuals, and the

86

break-ups can be far more disastrous, affecting as they do multitudes of people. Some of the factors that mar individual human love on a larger scale cause the disruption of relations between people and nations. There are national jealousies and hatreds as well as individual ones. Here, too, only when nations become divine will they have divine love for each other. The nation, like the individual, must become of a divine nature to love divinely. A spiritualized society must emerge if the torrents of international hate are to disappear and unity and peace take their place. Mankind is being impelled within toward such a society by his revulsion against the brutalities and excesses that continue to occur in present conditions.

Each individual and each nation must look upon every other individual and nation as a divine vessel, a portion of the Divine Being manifested on earth. They must have for each other the divine love of which Paul speaks in the superb passage in Corinthians: "Love is patient and kind; love is not jealous or boastful, it is not arrogant or rude. Love does not insist on its own way; it is not irritable or resentful; it does not rejoice at wrong, but rejoices at right. Love bears all things, hopes all things, endures all things, love never ends . . . Now faith, hope, and love abide; these three, but the greatest of these is love."[4]

How do we transform human love to the divine love of which Paul speaks? How do we cast the bitter fruit of egoism from human love? If such things as jealousy and the sorrow which it brings are still deeply rooted in your being, it is because you identify yourself with the ego and submit to the vehement cries and rashness of its impulses and demands. The remedy is to break off this identification. The ego is not the real you. You should take your stand in the soul, which is your real being, and the abode of divine love. Then you can eradicate jealousy and whatever else poisons love until at last they plague you no more. To do this it is necessary to aspire for the divine grace. You must remember that it is the force from above which is to transform all planes of your being and to transform humanity and the world society. To change your nature from the human to the divine requires more than your human power, and it is to this higher and divine force which we must call. Then our love will be like that which Christ commanded.

Christ said to his disciples, "Love ye one another as I have loved you." He was speaking as an incarnation of God, saying to them, "Love ye one another with a divine love."

---

[4] I Corinthians 13:1-13.

CHAPTER XI

HEALING THE SICK

HEALING THE SICK

In recent decades man has accelerated the healing of the sick, both by scientific and psychological methods. Some diseases he has either eliminated or reduced almost to the disappearing point, and he is waging the same campaign against those not yet conquered. In this effort he has discovered modern techniques, and evolved the art of healing by psychoanalysis.

Spiritual teachers have known for thousands of years that in the psyche is to be found the cause and the remedy for most sickness. The modern science of psychology has confirmed this ancient spiritual insight, and itself has proved a useful aid in the curative process. Psychology has not outmoded spiritual healing but confirmed and complemented it.

With the advent of modern medical science, spiritual healing became suspect. It went into eclipse. Faith healers were often looked on as charlatans preying on the sick. The modern miracles of medication and surgery were hailed as far more substantial and reliable for healing purposes than anything in the inner or spiritual realm. But only a few short decades ago a drastic change occurred. From within the ranks of science itself came the finding that most bodily disorders are induced by mental and emotional disturbances, and that many of them can be cured by clearing away these disturbances. The psychologists showed that, aside from accidental injuries, such as broken limbs, most hospital beds are filled by people whose sickness is of psychosomatic origin.

This type of illness or disability falls into four classes. First, there are those individuals whose nervous or emotional condition is so deteriorated that it causes them to feel painful symptoms of organic disease when laboratory tests prove that actually they have no disease; but they suffer, nevertheless, as if they had a physical illness. The suffering is real, though the disease is not.

Second, there are those individuals whose anxieties or nervous disturbances have been so acute and prolonged that they have actually lowered the bodily defenses and brought on disease by disorganizing the workings of the bodily apparatus. It is as if the directing hand had been removed from the bodily machine, allowing it to thrash about and wreck itself.

Third, there are those individuals who have indeed suffered accidental injury, but have delayed or hampered their lasting recovery due to their inner psychological maladjustments. In this third group there is a combination of accidental and psychosomatic illness, and here it becomes important to remedy the psychological cause in order to speed entire and permanent recovery from the accidental injury.

The fourth category is that of what is known as accident-prone people. Their inner being is so chaotically disturbed that accidents injurious to their body happen to them almost as if deliberately sought out.

Let us give an example of how inner disturbance causes sickness. Suppose an individual is so overwrought and inclined to panic that he cannot digest his food. As a result the body fails to get nutrition and strength from food properly assimilated. Consequently, disease occurs in some weakened portion or organ of the body. A bodily blight is caused. On the other hand, when by inner serenity these disturbances are quieted, the body again functions normally. It is uniformly nourished throughout, and maintained in a state of good health and vigor. With the removal of the inner disturbances, the outer symptoms disappear.

I have found by experience with this subject, it is always necessary at this point to inject a note of caution. Some people put all of their reliance on faith healing and none in doctors. Others go to the opposite extreme of relying only on doctors and giving no credence to faith healing. Both of these extreme attitudes are wrong. He who believes in self-healing will heal himself with divine grace. But he would be foolish to decline a surgical operation or medication prescribed by a doctor if necessary to save his health or life.

The great physician, Sir William Osler, said, "If all the medicine in the world were thrown into the sea, it would be good for the human race but bad for the fish." A similar statement was made by another doctor and published in the British Medical Journal. He said, "Good health is that state of physical well-being which is coupled with the liberation of an individual's maximum mental and physical capacity. Drugs have no part in promoting such a concept and they are foreign to its maintenance. What proportion of the population achieve 'good health' as thus defined is unknown, but is hardly likely to be a very large number."

We can agree with both of these doctors. The day will come when your inner defenses and spiritual knowledge are powerful enough to make you free of illness and reliance on drugs; but until that time you must be prepared to fall back on the doctor and his prescriptions when his help is needed, and be glad and thankful he is available. Yet, for maximum health, one should always endeavor to act from within on illness and cure it until he is safe and beyond the attacks of sickness.

What is essential is to go very thoroughly, very studiously, into the dialectic of spiritual healing. It is a great gift, a great power. Not everyone has it or can receive it. Christ healed spiritually where his disciples could not, as when he cured the lunatic boy after the disciples tried first and failed, and the scriptures say that Christ could do no mighty works such as his healings in his own home city because of the unbelief of the people there, to whom he was the carpenter's son, and not a teacher come from God.

The medical doctor sometimes has a difficult problem in diagnosing. He has trouble finding out just what it is that is making his patient sick. He follows a process of elimination; he checks every area and organ of the body. He runs laboratory tests and makes x-rays, until at last he finds the seat of the trouble. Then, with his diagnosis complete, he can begin treatment looking to cure. All the time he is working with concrete physical evidence, blood counts, electrocardiograms, etc.

In this respect, the methods of science can be profitably drawn on for spiritual healing; for in order to effect spiritual healing an even more meticulous and careful process must be followed. The diagnosis in spiritual cure is often elusive at first and the road to recovery exacting, but he who perseveres will heal himself. Here one is not dealing with physical evidence, such as blood counts and x-rays, which can be readily measured and seen. One is dealing with deep invisible thoughts, emotions, and psychic forces which do not show up on the fluoroscope or in laboratory reports. Nevertheless, as we have shown, in these mental, vital and psychic sources are to be found the cause and cure of most disease. Once we attain to mastery of this realm, of its own diagnostic and curative aspects, we possess a self-healing power which grows gradually or swiftly until we are immune from disease.

This is a healing force which medical science does not yet fully understand, although many noted doctors appreciate its importance. For instance, Sir William Osler said that in order to cure tuberculosis you should look into the mind, and not into the chest.

There is another contrast which makes spiritual healing the more arduous if also the most effective healing force. The doctor, in treating you, relies on his skill. The patient does not have much to do with it. If the doctor finds your gallbladder is diseased he will operate on you and remove the offending organ. Of course the doctor tries to get you to have an optimistic, cheerful attitude, for he realizes that will speed your recovery. Such a cheerful, optimistic, confident attitude is essential in spiritual healing also. So here the paths of the doctor and the psychic healer cross; they complement each other; both scalpel and prayer are working for the cure.

But in spiritual healing there is a dramatic difference. The individual, the one to be healed, has a much more important role. Christ made it a tremendously important role. Accounted a great healer himself in the spirit, he gave those whom he healed the credit, and not himself. "Your faith," he said, "has made you whole."

All great spiritual teachers have taught similarly. We are too prone to inertia, as Aurobindo says. We want to vegetate, to attach ourselves to the soil and the roots of safe anchorage, whether in regard to healing or otherwise. We cling servilely to custom and group suggestion when we should think and act for ourselves. We need a capacity for true freedom, an openness to novelty, a readiness "to seize intelligently and assimilate." Man needs to forgo his "downward propensity and earthward gaze" and raise his eyes upward to the Spirit and the Eternal whence his help and his healing descend. So in spiritual healing our openness, our faith, our knowledge, have a very important role.

"Fear of God," says the Talmud, "unlocks the outer door of the spiritual treasury, but it is knowledge that unlocks the inner door." There is such a thing as learning the ways of spiritual healing as there is learning the ways of medical healing.

We should do as Christ did. He did not confine himself to the four corners of the Old Testament in his day. Neither should we confine ourselves in our days to the four corners of the New Testament, or the Koran, or any other venerated scripture of the past. To do so would be to ignore and fail to take advantage of the increase in medical, psychological, and spiritual knowledge which has become available in the modern era. To do so would be to be lax in healing the sick. All sacred scriptures have antecedents, and will be followed by new scriptures which will be held equally sacred in the passage of time.

The older scriptures have relied on those which preceded them as their starting point. So must the new scriptures of the future, to be on solid base, proceed from what the great scriptures of realized thought and spiritual experience in the past have given to mankind.

Having presented the general outline of the subject, let us turn now to specifics of the inner cause and cure of disease. The chief cause of most diseases is that layer of mentality which psychologists call "the subconscious." The subconscious mind, as Aurobindo says, is an obscure reservoir of stubborn impressions, fixed notions, habitual reactions and desires, all of which control to a considerable extent the conditions of the body. It is the source from which illness generally arises. "Chronic or repeated illnesses are indeed mainly due to this inconscient and its obstinate memory and habit of repeating whatever has impressed itself upon the body as a reaction." It is the catch-basin for buried emotional tensions and conflicts which throw up disturbed and distorted reactions. These disturbances take habitual nerve paths already established to weakened portions of the body. So an individual automatically will get the same kind of illness over and over again from these concealed sources in the subconscious mind. They adopt any number of almost unrecognizable disguises.

Let us give an illustration of the subtlety of these disguises. An individual we will say, is consumed with personal ambition. He becomes ruthless, inconsiderate, vain, pompous, shallow, opportunistic. This spoils his relationships with others and ruins all his undertakings. Finally it begins to sap his health. Now thoroughly alarmed, he says to himself, "Something is wrong. I shall turn to religion. I will devote myself to God's work. In that way I will get rid of this ambition that is driving me to distraction. I will become a divine instrument, and fulfill the will of God."

This seems very good, but such a transfer in itself alone will not dispel the ambition. For he will find that ambition is no stranger to the pulpit, and not always absent in the priest. Such an individual, said Aurobindo, "will only replace the desire for one kind of fruit by the desire for another kind; he will strive more passionately perhaps for these higher results, and be more bitterly grieved by not attaining them. There is no passion so terrible as the passion of the altruist, no egoism so hard to shake as the fixed egoism of virtue, precisely because it is justified in its own eyes, and cannot see the necessity of yielding to a higher law . . . even if there is no grieving over the results, there will be incessant and passionate labor and strife, getting eager and getting exhausted, always under bondage . . ." As a result, he may bring upon himself a physical and spiritual downfall worse than anything he ever experienced before.

I have mentioned ambition only as an example. It could be anything else buried in the reservoir of the subconscious, such as hatred, haughtiness, malice, selfishness, resentment, envy.

Having discussed the inner cause of sicknesses, let us now consider how to heal them by spiritual force. For this we must aspire through the soul, the psychic being within us that stands in closeness to the Divine. We must bring the divine light into the obscure recesses of the subconscious mind, to reveal and disperse all its shadowy contents and subtle disguises, to throw off these masks. Then we see nothing anywhere except the Divine. We are at every moment one with God. We love Him in all beings and feel His joy in all things. We are moved only to help and to heal, to occupy ourselves with the good of all beings, to lead men to spiritual joy, to act for the progress of the world toward the Divine.

When our entire being is filled with the light, love, joy and power from above, all lower impulses and inferior motives and all their disguises are swept away, and with them go all the inner causes of sickness. We are then free of disease. Our life becomes divine.

Here also, however, nothing must creep in that will lessen this spiritual force, or cause us to mistake it, so that it cannot fully perform its healing work. Our love must be entire, cosmic. It must reach out to the Divine in all beings. Christ said we must love our enemies and the sinners who have committed transgressions. If we are to love the hostile and the sinful, shall we not also love the harmless and the innocent who happen to be ill-trained and ill-situated? As an ancient scripture of Judaism says, ''Into the house where the door is not open to the poor, the physician enters.'' The healing force that comes from God is all-loving, all-joyful, all-powerful, all-pure, all-compassionate.

As Aurobindo said, ''The remedy is to think constantly of the Divine, not of one's self; to work, act and do (your spiritual devotions) for the Divine, not to consider how this or that affects me personally, but to refer all to the Divine. It will take time to do that sincerely and thoroughly, but it is the proper way.''

''The whole principle is to open oneself to the divine influence. It is there above you and, if you can once become conscious of it, you have then to call it down into you. It descends into the mind and into the body as peace, as a light, as a force that works, as the presence of the Divine with or without form, as (bliss)."[1] It is this force that works in you and heals.

People tried to touch the garment of Christ. Knowing that the healing power from above was there, when they touched him, he could feel that healing power flow from him to them. The truth he taught sets men free from the bondage of sickness, as from every bondage. So did he say at the last to his disciples: "Go and teach all nations; heal the sick; and observe all that I have commanded you. And I will be with you to the end of the age."[2]

---

[1] Sri Aurobindo, *Bases of Yoga* (Pondicherry: Sri Aurobindo Press, 1955) pp. 39-40.
[2] Mat. 28:19-20.

CHAPTER XII

THE GODS OF MAN

THE GODS OF MAN

Man has had many gods and avatars whom he has worshipped, and whose personalities are as real to him as his own. Among them are Jehovah, Christ, Krishna, Buddha, Vishnu, Shiva, Brahma, Ahura-Mazda and many others. In addition to the true or higher gods, there are lesser gods and angels, such as Gabriel, Michael and Raphael, and titanic or demonic beings such as Lucifer, who, as the Bible says, fell from heaven like the morning star.

All of these populate the mystic realm of the gods. If temporal history is largely the biography of statesmen and warriors, religious chronicles are centered around the personalities and deeds of the gods and lesser supraphysical beings. The New Testament is an example, with its account of the birth and life of Christ, replete as it is with the acts of God, angels, spirits, demons, and of Christ himself.

The unbelieving and the anti-religious are apt to dismiss all this as so many myths by gifted story-tellers or superstitious priests. Yet none can deny that untold generations of men have found and still find these things to be valid by belief and by the test of experience in the crucible of the ages.

The existence of beings on higher and other planes beyond the human has not only been affirmed by humanity in the past, but in every new era including our own. New personalities are constantly being accepted as candidates for, or possessors of, this celestial status. In the Catholic Church, for instance, new saints are canonized, and men pray to them for intercession and aid on the spiritual plane. These new saints join others previously raised to similar position. In India many people have already made Gandhi an avatar. On a trip to India I saw his statues all over the country. I also found a similar elevation being extended to Sri Aurobindo by thousands of his disciples who look upon him as an avatar, and pray at his tomb even twenty-seven years now after his death, a constant stream of devotees from morning to night.

Anything of this kind which has persisted throughout the history of man, and is as vital and contemporary as ever, and is common to all races and climes, has acquired a subjective self-proof. It is as psychically real as anything physically real, and in fact far more so.

Science, which operates strictly in the physical, is constantly forced to modify its beliefs, axioms and concepts. In one century it may hold the earth to be flat, and in the next century round; at one time that space is limitless, and at a succeeding time that space curves back upon itself. In one era that there are three dimensions, and in the next that there are four dimensions; in one era it may rely on the theory of gravitation, in the next the theory of relativity. This is why the spiritual cannot base itself on science. If it did, every time science changes the whole metaphysical system would collapse. But spiritual truth is the same yesterday, today and forever, as the Bible says of Christ.

Yet, science too has its unseen forces, laws and principles. It gives them names such as "gravitation" and "relativity." Such principles become the ruling forces of the natural existence in the eyes of science.

The effects of their operation are tangible and practically utilized in daily life. Science also has what might be called its own brand of angelic and diabolic powers. There are, for instance, beneficent cells which preserve the health of the body, and malignant cells which tear it down. If a war goes on between the angels and the demons, according to the Bible, there is likewise a war in the physical, according to science.

The physical and its law are concrete to us because, as Aurobindo says, we are speaking of the material part of our consciousness. What is a law? It means a certain balance among universal forces under certain conditions. If you change the conditions you get a different result. It is not by a miracle that you change what you call a law.[1]

---

[1] A. B. Purani, *Evening Talks with Sri Aurobindo*, 2nd Series, pp. 285-286.

Now let us see what this quotation means. If consciousness is lowered to the animal realm, what happens? The conditions are different and the results are different. The animal cannot reason. He does not know the laws of logic, let alone the laws of spirit. The only law the animal knows is the law of instinct, and not that of the rational nor the supra-rational. The animal knows nothing of the mathematical equations of the mind or the gods and angels of the spirit.

Yet that does not mean that the equations do not exist or that the gods and angels do not exist. All it means is that the animal plane of lesser consciousness follows its own law and conditions. No miracle is going to happen whereby the animals will start building temples and founding religions. On the other hand, the human plane is at a higher level of consciousness and under its law and conditions man does build temples and worship God. But no miracle is going to happen here either. Present Man will not rise above his present plane. That will happen only when, in the words of Paul, man becomes a new creature of higher than present human consciousness. "You must be born again," said Christ. You must take on a super-manhood, a super-mentality, a Divine consciousness, instead of an animal or human consciousness. This new man in his consciousness will be as far above present man as present man is above the animal. Life which was once animalized, then humanized, will at last become divinized. Man himself will reach the plane of the gods.

The animal takes no thought that it will ever be more than an animal. Some men believe that they will never be more than man; that is the animal in them speaking. Men who are more developed mentally realize that they are to become divinized; that is the soul in them speaking. Man will not then be a god but he will be a Divine being. There are different planes of being in the spiritual as there are in the material. As Christ said, men will receive power to become the sons of God. Man's existence will then not be instinctual, like that of the animal, or mental like that of present man, but spiritual, like that of God.

Thus the Apostle Paul wrote in his letter to the Ephesians: "The Father, according to the riches of His glory . . . grant you to be strengthened with might through the spirit in the inner man, and that Christ may dwell in your hearts through faith; that you, being rooted and grounded in love may have power to comprehend with all the saints what is the breadth and length and height and depth, and to know the love of Christ which surpasses all knowledge, that you may be filled with all the fullness of God."[2]

---

[2] Ephesians 3:14-19.

The material plane is real. It is not going to disappear. But neither is it the only reality. As Aurobindo said, "I hope you don't believe that your physical self is the only being in you. These forces have their own plane and they are all the time busy with your earth plane. You must not exaggerate the importance of the earth-plane . . . it is not that it is not important. It is important according to what you put into it. Otherwise, how is the physical life of man better than that of an ant?. In order to bring down any higher spiritual force into the earth plane, you must sit down to it; you have to call down and hold the power in you. You have to allow it to organize your being and transform it. Then you can think of action."[3]

The struggle which the Bible describes as going on between angels and the demons is found in the scriptures of every religion. Mara, the evil one, tempted Buddha as he fasted forty days beneath the Bodhi tree where he became enlightened. Evil is the snake tempting Eve and causing Adam to fall before temptation in the Garden of Eden. It is a struggle as to who should control the destiny of man and the course of human evolution.

The world and man could have evolved differently, from glory to glory, like a flower blossoming from bud to bloom. But the divine purpose, which admits all possibilities, has permitted the satanic or evil force to interfere. Thus, man is to reach divine life by a struggle. Thus we will attain perfection and, as the Talmud says, "God will account him as worthy of great reward, as if he had done it all himself."[4]

What is our relationship to the plane of the gods and to angels and other supra-physical entities? The Bible says that God made man but little lower than the angels. The angels are on a fixed plane. They are typal, always the same; they are messengers or attendants upon God, bearing good tidings or warning man against evil, unsheathing the bright sword of the Divine against the satanic forces in the world. Man is of a different order. He is not a fixed type, but is evolving. If man is now but little lower than the angels, he is to rise beyond them to the sonship of God. It has been said of the lesser gods and angels that if they wished to go beyond their stationary or typal role they would have to become human in order to evolve. So if our life on earth has trials, it also has a promise of glory not given even to the angels and lesser deities. We are men that we shall become more than men and more than angels. Let us surmount our present difficulties that we may enjoy our future glories. God so loved us that He gave us life to perfect and the Divine to inherit.

[3] A. B. Purani, *Evening Talks with Sri Aurobindo*, First Series, pp. 279-280.
[4] A. B. Purani, *Evening Talks with Sri Aurobindo*, First Series, pp. 267-280.

Let us, however, keep a right perspective and our feet firmly planted on the earth. Man is not a god, as Aurobindo said, but he can attain to the plane of the gods, and there he has his divine self — the soul — which is a portion of the Divine. If you knock on their gates with desire, they show you on to the vital gods. By this is meant that you must approach the true gods without ego. If your approach is with ambition, lust, greed, or other egoistic preferences, you will go to the satanic entities who preside over these domains. They will fill you with what you want. The desire gods will give you inordinate economic wealth or unwarranted power over others, but only if you pay your debt to them, as Faust paid his to Mephistopheles.

The true gods and their avatars are aspects of the Supreme Divine Personality — God beyond all earthly planes, beyond all cosmic planes, beyond all celestial gods and hosts. Moses was such an aspect . . . the great lawgiver of justice, righteousness and mercy, as was Christ, the divine incarnation of love, and Buddha, the avatar of compassion.

"These are not mere abstractions," says Aurobindo. It is the mind that deals in abstractions, representations of realities of planes higher than the mind; behind these abstractions there is a reality. On the plane above the mind there are no abstractions , there are realities and powers. It is more intensely concrete than matter, something quite overwhelming in its concreteness . . . on that plane there is nothing more concrete than God. (So the Apostle Paul said that in God we live, move, and have our being.) Man is mostly on the physical plane now, and he thinks that the mind is more abstract than the body. When we are more highly developed mentally, the mind will be more concrete and real to us; and when we become spiritual, the Divine will be more concrete and real to us than either the abstractions of the mind or the materiality of the body. [5]

As to the form of the gods whom man has worshipped under many different names, they need not be human forms. The world is full of a complexity of forms. We see beauty and grace in many forms that are not human. So there is a sublime beauty of holiness in the Supreme Divine Personality who has no form and is yet the form of all things, and the delight of all beauty and loveliness.

We have two courses before us: We can depend upon our own willpower and energy. If so, we stay within the earth-plane. This is a lonely path, and whoever follows it must be their own refuge. A teacher can guide

[5] A. B. Purani, *Evening Talks with Sri Aurobindo*, First Series, p. 291.

you only to the refuge of yourself. To most people this course disappoints and leads nowhere; they desert or wander from it in the end. The other path is the one chosen by the great majority of individuals. It leads to the plane and refuge of the Supreme Divine, the Absolute of Absolutes, and to the help of His incarnations, prophets, and teachers. Their burden is easy and their yoke is light, and they bring peace to your mind and to your heart, as Christ said. If you rise to the plane and the refuge of the true gods, by whatever name you call them, then there will be divine light instead of human thought in your mind, divine love instead of human sentimentalism in your heart, divine power instead of human frailty in your body.

How do you ascend to the plane of the true gods? There is no set way. Nor will it be a miracle, but God working through your own nature. To begin with, you must realize that there is more to your being than your physical self, and you must sit down to the task and call down the divine consciousness and power and hold it in you. There are certain things which will prevent this. You cannot approach the Divine with egoism. All that has to go. You must be pure in heart and without arrogance. You must have faith in the new creation of yourself and of the world, as the prophet Isaiah said of God, "Behold, I create new heavens and a new earth, and the former things shall not be remembered or come into mind. Be glad and rejoice forever."

CHAPTER XIII

CONVERSION AND TRANSFORMATION

CONVERSION AND TRANSFORMATION

Conversion is usually considered that process by which the individual becomes religious, is changed, and feels a grace and security he had not possessed before. Where previously he was in conflict within himself and unhappy, he becomes triumphantly unified and joyful. His new-found belief gives him a cosmological explanation of the universe; he feels at last that he has discovered reality.

Some psychologists have claimed that intrinsically conversion is an ordinary occurrence of the adolescent period of human life. As such, they say, it is a concomitant of the transition from the little universe of the child to the broader mental and spiritual life of the mature individual.

It may be, they say, that theology has utilized this adolescent tendency to bring individuals into the deeper comprehension of the mature adult. This psychological observation no doubt has an element of fact in it which helps us to understand conversion; but there is a deeper spiritual truth of conversion and transformation. This does not lessen the usefullness of the complementary knowledge that psychology furnishes on this subject. After all, Paul himself said that when he was a child he thought as a child and spoke as a child, but when he became a man he put away childish things. Yet, for the profoundest understanding of this matter, we must turn to spiritual knowledge, for this is a spiritual subject.

Conversion, as it is usually understood today, means that a person resolves or decides to become an adherent of a certain religion or to follow a particular path of spiritual attainment. It is a decision, an act of the will. When the person makes that decision, a vast field of change in their life stretches before them to be undertaken through their efforts with the aid of Divine Grace. This change is transformation. If conversion is the decision, transformation is the fulfillment of the decision, the achievement of spiritual realization, the arrival of the individual at liberation and perfection, oneness with the Divine. That is the supreme Godward movement of man's life and the object of his existence.

Conversion is a term not so much used in the Orient as it is in the West. It is the West from which missionaries have gone forth in large numbers in recent centuries in an effort to convert people in other parts of the world. In modern Eastern spiritual teachings, conversion is considered as the will to change, as a first step toward inner transformation. This will to change can be adopted very quickly, or on the moment.

However, transformation is a different matter; by transformation man attains his perfection and his highest spiritual good. In the Orient the usual opinion is that thirty-five years is generally required for the individual to achieve it.

In the ancient Judeo-Christian tradition, the ardor of the the change was likewise fully recognized. Christ said that hard is the road and narow the way that leads to life eternal, and few there be that find it.

The classic example of sudden conversion in Christianity is that of Paul on the road to Damascus. He had a vision which instantly changed him from a persecutor to an apostle of Christ. But that did not mean that he was instantly transformed in his being; he had to go to the desert to meditate. Later he said that he had still not perfected himself, but was working toward perfection. Paul's conversion was sudden but his transformation was slow. Of his conversion Paul was sure; but he was equally sure that, resplendent as his vision was, and fixed as his conversion turned out to be, he had not yet transformed himself. On this he was to work for much, if not all the rest of his life.

Western religion now needs to make a clear distinction between conversion and transformation. Its chief emphasis now is on conversion, the lesser of the two, instead of on transformation, which is the greater. The West needs to revitalize and re-apply its valid ancient teachings concerning transformation. This is the rebirth which Christ said is necessary to enter the Kingdom of God.

Where Christ and Paul taught that the way to this goal is hard and the time protracted, the modern Western religious tendency is to reduce it to the comparatively effortless and brief act of conversion, as merely the making of a decision. Most evangelistic crusades in this country today are decision campaigns.

The modern Western requirements for conversion vary; but they are alike in that the time required is short, or waived altogether. Some instruction, generally brief, is given as to the creed or doctrines of the particular church.

Catholics require the novice to take instructions before he is accepted as a convert to Catholicism. Many Protestant denominations, on the other hand, accept converts immediately as communicants with no instruction or probationary period required. Protestants sometimes conduct follow-up campaigns to help the convert in his spiritual aspiration, and have periodic revivals for the same purpose.

Human history shows that questions have always arisen concerning these processes. Conversion to a religion has never been automatically considered a religious virtue. Objections have been made and doubts voiced as to the authenticity of the religion to which the person is converted, and as to the depth, scope, genuineness, and constancy of the conversion. All of us know from ordinary human experience, that conversion from one religion to another is frequently the cause of conflicts within families and of the rupture of friendships. The religions themselves do not deem all conversion praiseworthy. The Catholic Church for long centuries bitterly fought against and condemned as irreligious the conversion of Catholics to Protestantism, and Protestant denominations have been divided among themselves on this score.

A leading national Methodist Church official recently was quoted in the press as scoffing at what he called "quick conversion to Christianity," saying that people come slowly to God, even if it sometimes appears otherwise. He said that the quick converters take a fragment of the gospel and say this is the whole gospel; they don't, he said, give a full rounded interpretation of the gospel of Christ.

I have had some experience at rapid-fire conversion on a large scale. In my early ministry that was my principal work on behalf of a national Protestant denomination, and later independently. Once I led 500 people to conversion in a year, when I was only 22 years old and barely able to vote. I went from place to place, assembled people, preached to them and called for

111

converts to come to the altar. Now I am a few years older and I would consider it a remarkable achievement if, in one year, I were able to help a handful of people to their own transformation. For by that change, the perfection of the soul manifests itself in the mind, heart and life of the individual. Nevertheless, I know of some people who have been spiritually helped by quick-decision conversion. It would be wrong to take this method away from those whom it has so helped, or will help.

I became convinced, however, that even if this helped some, it is not the most effective or highest path to transformation, either for the individual or mankind. There seemed to be too much emphasis on how many came forward to be saved, and not enough on the tremendous self-change that salvation demands. I came to see that it was not the number of converts but the quality of the conversion that counted.

Another factor also entered: It became untenable to me to say that conversion and ensuing transformation could be effected only through one particular religion, or still more narrowly, through only one sect of that religion. I could find nothing in God, Christ, or the Divine Truth that would justify me in continuing to tell men that they would be excluded from divine salvation unless they accepted what I preached and nothing else. I became convinced that their best teacher was not myself or any other evangelist, but the Divine Spirit that Christ and Paul said dwell within them, the portion of the Godhead in them and in all.

I saw that the truly converted and the truly transformed, the great in soul, are those who open themselves to the "light and the largeness of which the divine nature in man is capable." It is these great-souled ones only who are "on the path narrow in the beginning, but inexpressibly wide in the end," which leads to perfection and the immortal. "The growth of God in man is man's proper business," "The steadfast turning of man's lower nature into the Divine nature" is the subject of transformation and the secret meaning of human existence.[1]

When, by the grace of God, these insights came to me, it became impossible for me to go on with the kind of restrictive conversion ministry in which I had been engaged, regardless of the success which others seemed to think I had reached in these labors. The upshot was that to the considerable consternation of my friends and associates, and over their protests, I left this type of evangelical work, to go to the new work in which I am now engaged, in accordance with the Divine command.

---

[1] Anilbaran Roy, *The Gita* (Pondicherry; Sri Aurobindo Ashram Press, 1954) pp. 147-148.

In addition to the reasons that I have already cited for this action, I realized that while I, myself, had been a religious convert from my earliest years, I had yet to seek and achieve my own transformation and to fortify my faith with spiritual knowledge. Only by endeavoring to do so myself could I preach to others that they should do likewise. Like Paul, I cannot say that I have become perfect, but am working toward perfection. As Aurobindo once said, "Whoever sincerely seeks the spiritual transformation can teach of it to others, even if he has not yet fully or adequately attained it himself. It is only if he is insincere that he is a hypocrite."

Permit me to speak further of my own experience in this respect, and that of my father, who was a minister before me. He knew, as many other ministers know, that a number of people who come forward at religious crusades to announce their conversion have done so over and over again at revival meetings.

My father nearly broke up a serious church conference once when the annual reports were being given. One minister reported that he had made 100 converts in his church that year. My father, from whom I expect I inherited some independence, got up and inquired: "What does that mean — 25 four times over?" The stress was being put in the wrong place. If the stress had been placed on transformation, perhaps the 25 might not have had to come to the altar four times over to repeat their conversions. Such a process of repeated conversion sometimes engenders a feeling of guilt and failure instead of progress toward transformation. I have had people tell me this and say they had failed and sinned against the Holy Spirit. They felt that they still were not saved, for they still had the same problems, and said that it was useless for them to go to the altar any more.

Our object should be not conversion alone, but transformation. Or, to put it another way, it is that conversion which is transformation, the rebirth spoken of by Christ. We should make no insistence on particular beliefs, forms or ceremonies, recognizing that men are differently drawn in these respects according to their temperament and traditions. We should regard as essential the spiritual conversion that is lived out, and whatever form or opinion into which it is cast may naturally vary. This transformation must be inwardly lived by each individual, and it will then also become realized in the external life of mankind.

We cannot approach the Divine Presence without the greatest preparation and change in ourselves, of which man is capable by Divine Grace. All dross must be tempered out of us in this working until God acts in and through us to establish His glory upon the earth.

The problem of how to take the convert and make a transformed being of him has always been a major one in every religion or spiritual system. Paul spent much time converting men or gaining souls, and as much or more time holding or changing those whom he gained. This is the theme of his great Epistles. Paul's letters are not written to unbelievers, or to the unconverted; they are addressed to the churches, to believers, and the converted who need strengthening, fashioning, moulding into true images of Christ to whom they had pledged their allegiance. Sometimes the appeal in his letters is urgent and stern, as well as loving. Paul worked as hard on converting the converted as he did on making new converts. His aim was to change converts into spiritual beings. His work with them only began when he converted them.

His first letter to the Corinthian converts is an example. Paul told them he had heard there was immorality and arrogance among them; he warned them against malice and evil, against drunkenness and debauchery. [2] He sought to elevate not only their morals but their intelligence and their spiritual insight.

"Brethren," he wrote, "be not children in your thinking; be babes in evil, but in thinking be mature."[3] Yet, "among the mature," he continued, "do we impart wisdom, although it is not a wisdom of this age or the rulers of this age which are doomed to pass away. But we impart a secret and hidden wisdom of God which God decreed before the ages for our glorification . . . that your faith might rest not in the wisdom of man, but in the power of God."[4]

Religion has always called for faith, love and works; now it should call as strongly for divine knowledge, as Paul did, so that all of these are raised beyond themselves to the *divinest significance*. Thus do we rise to the highest love of God which the Bible says is the first and greatest commandment; for as that commandment says, you should love God with all your mind, heart and might; that is, with intelligence, feeling and power.

Our modern religious crusades tend to call strongly for faith, but only weakly for knowledge, but faith is strongest and in the light when it has knowledge among its companions. An announcement that so many people have been converted in a religious crusade is not the test of its effect. The only effective test, the only true gauge of any conversion, is whether a

---

[2] I Cor. 5:1-2, 6-8.
[3] I Cir 14:20.
[4] Ibid. 2:5-7

114

transformation occurs by which the Divine "takes up our nature into His" and fills it "with His own knowledge and power." Only then the Divine "lays His hands on our obscure ignorant nature," and changes it into His own light and wideness.[5]

In this approach we open ourselves to that knowledge and power from above. In our sermons, lectures, classes and publications, it is our endeavor that there be no obscurity, insubstantiality, or weakness in what we say or teach, but the full measure of the divine light and glory. This we also try to do even in our work with children, so that they may discover the truth at the earliest age, and walk, as Paul said, not as unwise but as wise men and women, filled with the Spirit.

Christ said, "Let not your heart be troubled; you believe in God, believe also in me. In my Father's house are many mansions; if it were not so I would have told you. I go to prepare a place for you and if I go I will come again, and receive you unto myself, that where I am you may be also; and where I go you know and the Way you know."

Thus did Christ say that we must have preparation in order to have a place in the house of God, that we might be as He is, and that we know this is the Way. And when Thomas asked, "How can we know the Way?" Christ replied, "I am the Way, the Truth, and the Life."

And so the path to the Eternal is through the Truth.

---

[5] Op. cit.

CHAPTER XIV

THE RESURRECTION

THE RESURRECTION

Throngs of reverent people assemble in a sacred place of worship to commemorate the resurrection of Christ on Easter. The career, crucifixion and resurrection of Christ are not only the principal events of human history to Christianity, innumerable non-Christians, also, venerate Christ; they recognize him, if not as sole Savior, then as one of the few incarnations of the Divine and deliverers of mankind. Thus, Easter is rightly a day of universal holiness.

By the time of Christ, and long before he lived, the belief in resurrection had become widely accepted among the Jews. Resurrection to them was the doctrine of the reunion of the soul and the body after death. This is not the same thing as belief in the immortality of the soul, and "the eternal survival of human personality." It means that the body, spiritualized and purified, takes on immortality also. Eternality of the individual under this doctrine is not that of a disembodied soul, but of the soul and the perfected body in which it dwells.

Resurrection became one of the cardinal tenets of the Christian creed. To it is due much of the enormous expansion of Christianity through the 2,000 years of its history, for the doctrine responds to one of the fondest hopes of the heart, the belief that in some way the personality of the body which the soul inhabits shall, like the soul, become pure and eternal. This Christian promise of the integral immortality of spirit and form came as an answer to the mystery of existence, and as deliverance from the vicissitudes of earthly life. Multitudes of men become converts to the religion that gave them this comfort and assurance.

It is more and not less a confirmation of the belief in resurrection that it is not peculiar to Christianity. It is found in Zoroastrianism, as well as in later Judaism for centuries before Christ was born.

The Hebrews whom Moses led out of Egypt possessed an intermixed culture in which Hebrew, Egyptian and Canaanite elements occurred. Their religion was already an advanced ethical monotheism, as laid down by the great law-giver, Moses. Egypt was an ancient center of culture and knowledge, and Moses was not only a Hebrew, but also an Egyptian prince, a man of profound spiritual knowledge and wide education.

In the commandments, statutes and ordinances of Moses, as recorded in the Bible in early Judaism, there is no emphasis on resurrection. There is no mention at all of resurrection in the Ten Commandments, the central feature of the Mosaic Law. On the other hand, resurrection is a paramount doctrine in the formal creed of Christianity. Yet, as we shall see, it was from later Judaism that Christianity was to derive the resurrection belief.

After the death of Moses, the Hebrews under Joshua stood in battle array against the gates of Canaan. There they came into contact with a kind of resurrection doctrine in the Canaanite religion of the god Baal. It was a cyclic theory. The gods of Canaan were fertility gods and sex worship had an important place in the Baal religion. The cycle was Spring, Summer, Fall and Winter. The rains fell, the summer harvest came, then the fall and winter. The god Baal was slain every fall — that is the meaning of the word "fall" — and resurrected every spring.

To the monotheistic Hebrews, the religion of Canaan with its annual slaying, the resurrection of "god," and its sex worship, was an abomination, and it is so termed in the Old Testament. Joshua and the prophets warned the Hebrews to stay faithful to the one living God of Judiasm, and to abhor Baal.

After the Jews returned from exile in Babylon, however, the belief in resurrection appeared in later Judaism, under the influence of the Zoroastrianism of Persia, but it is not the cyclic resurrection of Canaan with its yearly slaying of God and exhaltation of sex, it is a promise of eternal life through the grace of God, a resurrection compatible with the lofty monotheism of the Hebrews. An example may be seen in the verses of the prophet Isaiah written seven hundred years before Christ: "Thy dead shall live, their bodies shall rise. O dwellers in the dust, awake and sing for joy."[1]

---

[1] Isaiah 26:19

And again Isaiah says that God will swallow up death forever and wipe away tears from all faces.[2]

The Prophet Hosea spoke these verses: "Where is thy sting, O Death, where is thy doom, O Grave?" — words that were to be echoed centuries later by the Apostle Paul. The resurrection belief is found also in other books of the Old Testmanet, in Job, Ezekiel, Daniel, and the Psalms.

By the time of Christ, this more elevated doctrine of resurrection was widely accepted by the Pharisees, the largest and most progressive sect among the Jews, although rejected by the Sadducees. It was in an attempt to trap Christ on this doctrine that some of the Sadducees asked Christ the question about the woman who married seven brothers, one after the other: "At the resurrection, to whom will she be wife?" Christ gave his answer: "At the resurrection they shall neither marry nor be given in marriage; they will be as angels in heaven."[3]

The belief of the Pharisees in resurrection was to save Paul when he was on trial before the council, as related in the Book of Acts in the New Testament. "Brethren," said Paul, "I am a Pharisee, a son of Pharisees, with respect to the hope of the resurrection of the dead I am on trial." And when he had said this, a dissension arose between the Pharisees and the Sadducees, and the assembly was divided; for the Sadduces say there is no resurrection, nor angel, nor spirit; but the Pharisees acknowledge them all. Then a great clamor arose, and some of the scribes of the Pharisees' party stood up and contended: "We find nothing wrong in this man. What if an angel or spirit spoke to him?"

Later, when Paul was brought before King Agrippa, Paul made bold to say to the King, "You are familiar with the customs and controversies of the Jews. King Agrippa, do you believe the prophets? I know that you believe."[4] Here Paul was referring to declarations such as those of Isaiah and other prophets, proclaiming the raising of the dead. King Agrippa did not deny that he believed, but he kept out of that controversy between his subjects by answering Paul obliquely, saying, "In a short time you think to make me a Christian."[5] Such was the history and the status of the belief in resurrection among the Jewish people, parties, and rulers of Palestine during the lifetime of Christ and Paul.

---

[2] Ibid., 25:8.
[3] Mat. 22:23-32
[4] Ibid. 26:27
[5] Acts 26:28

Christ made certain vital additions to the resurrection doctrine which Paul was to promulgate throughout the Mediterranean world. Before describing these additions, we should first note some interpretations of various Christian sects not long after the crucifixion. Just as the Jews had adopted and developed a resurrection belief different from that of the Canaanites, the various Christian denominations differed among themselves regarding this doctrine. Their disparate theories ranged from those who called themselves Christians, but did not believe in resurrection at all, to those who believe in it according to the letter of the New Testament. Among the believers, themselves, however, serious rifts arose because of varying interpretations.

For instance, some Christians held that Christ was crucified not as the Son of God, but as a human being and not God. They asserted that God cannot die as Christ did on the cross, since God does not die, even temporarily, to be resurrected thereafter. Others declared that Christ was Very God, even in his death on the cross, and was resurrected thereafter. Yet it is actually unnecessary to find conflict in such controversies. There are elements of truth in both of these doctrines, as there is in every religious belief, and all can be reconciled in the spiritual oneness.

It is true that God does not die even temporarily, for He is Absolute, Eternal Existence. But it is also true that God can incarnate, and that while the human form of the incarnation might perish, the soul, the spirit of God within the human body, does not perish on the cross or otherwise. It is eternal and imperishable; so there is no substantial conflict in these varying interpretations.

Having thus harmonized such doctrinal disputes, let us now turn to what Christ and Paul have to say. By the time of Christ the rabbis in their academies were advancing the resurrection doctrine, yet further than the prophets of the past. They said in the Talmud: "This world is like a vestibule before the world to come; prepare thself that thou mayest enter into the hall. Better is one hour of repentance and good deeds in this world than the whole life of the world to come; and better is one hour of blissfulness of spirit in the world to come than the whole life of this world."[6]

These sayings seem almost as hard to understand as some of the sayings and parables of Christ. They are profound but not paradoxical. What these Judaic sages were intimating is that this world and its life should not be neglected, and that the bliss of the world to come could be attained in

---

[6]Ethics of the Fathers IV:21-22.

this natural world. The line of distinction between the present and the future world seems to fade away.

Christ was prepared to go yet further. He said to Martha, "I am the resurrection and the life." Note here how he connects the two — resurrection, and also life. Christ continued, "He who believes in me, though he die, yet shall he live; and whoever lives and believes in me shall never die."[7] These two statements are not made before in the scriptures. The first was familiar enough; he who died would by faith be raised or resurrected to life in the next world. But the second was new, and in it Christ seemed clearly to declare that those who believe in him would not die at all; they would receive earthly immortality.

Previously the Bible had spoken of only two men who did not die: Enoch, who walked with God,[8] and the Prophet Elijah.[9] According to the Old Testament scriptures, God took both of them directly from earth to heaven, and they did not see death. The Apostle Paul repeats this regarding Enoch.[10] This is what is called "translation" — passage from this world to the next without dying. It is not the earthly immortality which Christ intimates; he does not speak of translation, but life eternal, and not for two men only, but for all men.

After Christ himself, no one expounded the new teaching as ably as his great Apostle Paul. Paul compared first or present man with the future man, or new creature who is to be. In a letter to the Corinthians, Paul wrote these words: "The first man, Adam, became a living being; the last Adam became a life-giving spirit. But it is not the spiritual which is first, but the physical, and then the spiritual. The first man was from the earth, a man of dust; the second man is from heaven. As was the man of dust, so are those who are of the dust, and as is the man of heaven, so are those who are of heaven. Just as we have borne the image of the man of dust, we shall also bear the image of the man of heaven[11]. . . as sure as there is a physical body," said Paul, "so also is there a spiritual body."[12]

Thus from the dust, from the dim mind of the animal, from the half-light of the present mind of man, man in the future shall rise to the full light

---

[7] John 11:25-26.
[8] Gen. 5:24.
[9] II Kings 2:11.
[10] Heb. 11:5.
[11] I Cor. 15:45-50.
[12] Ibid. 15:42-44.

of the divine gnosis to what Paul calls the *Mind of Christ*, the mature wisdom of God. Human man is to become divine man, and divine man is to have a divine body.

"Christ was resurrected," said Paul, "that we too might walk in the newness of life. Our old self was crucified with him," declares Paul, "that we might be freed from wrong-doing. So you also," he said, "must consider yourself dead to sin, and alive to God. Do not yield your members as instruments of wickedness," said Paul, "but yield yourselves to God as men who have been brought from death to life, and your members to God as instruments of righteousness."[13]

Paul realized that these teachings were not easy to comprehend. "I am speaking in human terms because of your natural limitations," he said, ". . . for the wages of sin is death, but the free gift of God is eternal life in Christ."[14]

Thus there can be discerned the gradual unfolding of the principle of resurrection and immortality in the religions of man. From the primititive resurrection of the Canaanites to the lofty verses of Isaiah that God shall swallow up death and wipe away tears from all faces, to the promise of Christ that man shall not perish but have everlasting life, to the words of Paul, "O Death, where is thy sting, O Grave, where is thy victory?" — this unfoldment rises until it reaches the summit of perfection and earthly immortality expressed by Christ for the new divine manhood on earth.

The Kingdom of God that Christ said is within you, is to be realized also in the external existence. As surely as there is now an imperfect society ruled by the human mind, so shall there be a perfect society ruled by the soul.

The grand principle of resurrection and immortality, as it grows and widens in Judeo-Christian spirituality, is not the reincarnation, such as believed in Buddhism. In that Indian religion the soul transmigrates from body to body until perfection is reached. At that point there is an end of the individual's conscious existence. The personality is annihilated by absorption in nirvana. This is a last farewell to life, a permanent exit from natural conditions, an end to embodied existence. It is not immortality, but annihilation in the void and the silence.

---

[13] Romans 6:6-14.
[14] Ibid. 6:17, 19, 23.

The principle of resurrection is the opposite; it is a reflection of divine reality, both in spirit and in form. God not only exists as truth and spirit, but as concrete form in nature. Man, likewise, has the spirit of God within him, and a natural body. The ultimate aim of the resurrection principle is not to annihilate the life and the body, but to unite them with the soul in perfect divinized form.

As most people still understand and believe it, resurrection is to occur after death, so that the giving up of life occurs even if only temporarily; but man aspires to be free of death, even as God is free. He has always sought to go beyond the veil of the transient to the eternal abode of victory. To die and return is for man a conquest of a sort; but there is a greater victory, and that is not to die, to rout the foe altogether and without even a temporary defeat.

In the words of Christ, there is the hint and the foretelling of the evolution of man to earthly immortality. Life shall not be given up at all; death will be swallowed up, as Isaish said.

All that is unique and beautiful in the individual life shall be divinized and glorified. The love, beauty, kindness, valor, compassion, gentleness, personality and physique of the individual shall become pure and perfected in form, and shall inherit the earth, as Christ said. The body shall become a perfect expression of the soul, possessed of the joy and beauty of the spirit. Man's knowledge will not rest from its labors until all barriers are passed. Even in his natural existence, the veil that separates him from the Divine must be sundered.

Man from the most ancient times has believed that he has a destiny beyond death; he now has the higher aim of a destiny that eludes death like the bright divine beings who have tasted the nectar of immorality. Created by the Lord, but little lower than the angels, as the Bible says, man would now climb above the fixed plane of the angelic hosts. Pure and eternal in spirit already, he would be pure and eternal in body also. If, by the grace of God, he rises from death by the same power, he need not succumb to death at all.

In retrospect, nothing could seem more unbelievable and incredible than the evolutionary rise of man from the dust of the earth to the reasoning human mind of today, so far has the spirit within man taken him already; but this is not the end of the journey of the soul or the summit of man's attainment. All past human advance will seem minor as, under the homing urge of the soul, man rises from perfection to perfection, from glory to glory, until reunited within the Divine.

"I am the resurrection and the life," Christ said, "he who believes in me shall not perish but see life everlasting." "Eye has not seen," says the Bible, "nor ear heard, nor the heart of man conceived what God has prepared for those who love Him and works for those who wait for Him."[15]

---

[15] I Cor. 2:9, Isaiah 64:4, 65:17-18.

CHAPTER XV

THE CHANGE IN CONSCIOUSNESS

THE CHANGE IN CONSCIOUSNESS

For the future of the world a change in consciousness is necessary. We have the choice as to whether we will work together to effect this change voluntarily and peacefully. If we elect not to do so, then experience proves that it will be forced on us involuntarily and in the throes of catastrophe. It has been said that stronger than an army is an idea whose time has come; and much stronger than a timely idea is the change in consciousness which Nature and the Divine have prepared.

Let us take an example from the history of our own country: A century ago the level of human consciousness in some large portions of the United States, and among many people of those areas, was not one in which the inner principle of equality prevailed. As a result, one race was permitted to enslave another and insisted on the preservation of that privilege. The result was a resort to force, through which the outer institution of slavery was abolished by the awful catastrophe of the Civil War.

Nor did the Civil War fully solve the problem, as time has shown. Outer slavery went but inner inequality remained. The social institution changed but the inner consciousness did not. The Constitution was amended to prohibit involuntary servitude, but the consciousness of many people both North and South did not change from inequality to equality. The result has been the civil and human rights struggle of today. Unless this inner change does occur in the consciousness, in the spirit, catastrophe could be forced on us from this source in the 20th Century, as it was in the 19th. But fortunately the signs are that this inner change is developing. It will provide the basis for any necessary additional laws and external rearrangements against racial discrimination. The climate of consciousness is different today than it was a century ago.

This example from our nation's history is an illustration of a universal principle. Its application is necessary to the solutions of the profoundest human problems, including the question of human unity, freedom, and world peace, which are so pressing today. As in the case of American race equality, "no general peace can come to this anxious world" without a change in consciousness. This does not signify that outer measures are unnecessary. Constitutional amendments against slavery and laws against racial discrimination, and organizations such as the United Nations, to keep peace in the world, will be required. These measures will restrain the heartless until the heart and consciousness of mankind is changed. Then beyond all outer compulsions his consciousness will spontaneously guide him in the paths of equality, harmony, and liberation.

How is it possible for consciousness to become such that humanity is one in spirit? How can the consciousness of human unity grow? What will be the result for human life on earth through such a change in consciousness? Let us begin by finding what change of consciousness is. Most of us know that there are different kinds of consciousness, some lower or higher, some hidden and some more revealed, some about which little is known and some about which more is known or will be known. The modern science of psychology has made this more or less generally understood. It has defined different grades of consciousness, such as the unconscious, subconscious, conscious, and super-conscious. So one cannot say "consciousness is consciousness," and let it go at that, any more than one can say "mind is mind and that is all." There are different degrees of rationality; some people are more developed rationally than others, as we all know. Consciousness, which is a higher power than mind, likewise has developed to higher planes; it has been more and more realized and disclosed. It is the consciousness emerging from within which has energized the development of the mind and other faculties of man.

Consciousness is everywhere in different degrees of expression. If the Divine is admitted at all, His consciousness must be involved in all things, and by Its nature must seek Its perfect unveiling. The beginning of evolution is the involution of the divine existence in matter. There was a time when matter was considered dull, inanimate, lifeless; but science has radically altered that view. Religion long ago knew this secret. Genesis opens the Bible by describing man's creation as a breathing of the divine spirit into the dust, by which Adam was made a conscious being, a living soul.

Science has shown that seemingly motionless and inanimate matter contains intricate nuclear worlds in movement and vibration, with precise orbits and coordination, miniature galaxies and microscopic universes. It is a fluidity of force condensed in a particular form, just as man's body is a particular condensation of consciousness in materiality. But consciousness in matter is deeply hidden and veiled.

Next there emerged forms of cellular primitive life with a low degree of consciousness. Then the animals appeared, which possess a more developed consciousness. Next, in man, as Aurobindo says, the energizing consciousness appears as mind more clearly aware of itself and things. This is still a limited and a partial, not an integral power of itself, but a first conceptive potentiality and promise of integral emergence is visible. That integral emergence is the goal of evolving nature. It is the change of consciousness which man must attain to realize fully the soul and the divine existence in the world.[1]

Our first business in the universe is to affirm ourselves, but we also have to evolve and exceed ourselves. We must "expand our partial being into a complete being, our partial consciousness into an integral consciousness. We have to achieve not only mastery of his individual environment, but also world unity and world harmony. We have to realize and fulfill our individuality, but also expand it into 'a cosmic self' and a universal and spiritual delight of existence."[2]

In man's present mentality there is much that is obscure, wrong and ignorant. This must be transformed, chastened, corrected. Blessed is the man, says the Psalm, whom the Lord chastens. Through these changes man must ultimately reach a "free and wide harmony and luminousness of knowledge, will, feeling, action and character. Such is the plain intention of man's nature. It is the ideal that we acknowledge and aim for, which the creative energy has set before our intelligence."[3]

Thus we must attain a new power of existence, a consciousness beyond our mentality. It is this which Christ meant when he told men they must be born again, become new creatures, in order to enter the Kingdom of God. This is the hope of our life in the midst of the natural occurrences of the universe.

---

[1] Sri Aurobindo, *The Life Divine*, Ch. XVII.
[2] Ibid.
[3] Ibid.

Now principally an external being, we are transient in the short years of our life, as Shakespeare says: "Out, brief candle," and our life flickers away. We are now subject to the vicissitudes and restraints of our environment and closed inside our limited mentality.

Now how is our consciousness to change? How will we differ from present chiefly external man? He has to become *the real inner man* who is master of himself and his environment, universal in his being, limitless in his intelligence. The natural man is the past product of the evolutionary nature and the involution of the divine consciousness in nature, the breathing of the breath of God into man. He must become the divine man by the complete evolution of that consciousness. "The sons of Death have to know themselves as the children of Immortality." This is what justifies the human birth as a turning point in evolution and a critical event in the nature of the world. It is the purpose which Christ saw in the advent and the ascent of humanity. "Be born again," he said; "receive power to become the sons of God; you shall not perish but see life everlasting." This is the message which all people must hear, the ideal they must seek, and the consciousness to which they must change.

The new knowledge at which we must arrive is not a mental knowledge. The mind cannot make us children of immortality and sons of God. "A mental conception of God and ourselves and the world," says Aurobindo, "is an object good for the intellect but not large enough for the spirit; it will not make men conscious sons of the Infinite." It should be our aim to "be, to become, the highest that we know." This is the real knowledge.[4] It is knowledge such as Christ had, and at which his listeners marveled, and said: "How does this man know letters, having never learned?" and Christ answered and said, "My doctrine is not mine, but His that sent me."[5]

The next question is how to grow into the higher consciousness. To do so we must be aware of our real being, the soul, and possess and live in it so that it is expressed in our outer life, in real and unending joy. Once we understand this to be our object through the intelligence, we must fix the determination to achieve it in our will, and aspire to it in our soul. "Ask, and you shall be given," said Christ, "Knock and the door will be opened." Only now you know what to ask, and on which door to knock. All these elements are necessary — the knowledge to see, the will to persevere, and

---

[4]Sri Aurobindo, *The Life Divine,* Ch. XVII.
[5]John 7:15-16.

the soul's aspiration. Thus man attains liberation. It is the good pleasure of the Divine to give this salvation to us.

The final question is: What will be the result of this change in consciousness? How will things differ from what they now are? Before replying to this query, it will be well to note and to refute the argument of those who contend that consciousness in no way affects the conditions of man and the world, either favorably or adversely. That is the basic and erroneous theory of Communist dialectic. Karl Marx wrote these words: "It is not the consciousness of men that determines their existence, but on the contrary their social existence determines their consciousness." It is because of this fallacious proposition that Communist nations have a deep antipathy against all religion and do their utmost to extinguish it.

What consciousness has Communism determined? It set out to unite the proletariat. Yet the worst exchanges of vituperation and the greatest disunity in the world today is between Communist nations. The last thing that Marx expected — a terrible war between Communist nations professing his doctrines — is now considered a possibility. Communism, for all of its theories of the determinative function of the outer existence, has failed to lead men toward unity and peace. This is the basic flaw in the beliefs of Marxian Communism. This is why Communism is a dying creed, no matter how externally strong it may still seem or may continue to be for a time.

Now there may be considered the results of the change in consciousness. The natural world will be changed. A change of consciousness does not at all mean something that is to happen only transcendentally or in another world and that has nothing to do with this natural world. There are those who, seeking to defend the spiritual, declare that there can be no ground of compromise or co-existence between Communism and a transcendent spiritual order. That is true, but it is not the entire or integral truth, and by what it omits, it puts the free religious world at a dangerous disadvantage. It leaves Communism firmly entrenched on its own ground in the natural world, which is the only one Communism acknowledges or cares about. On this point also a successful defense against Communism can and must be waged, so that it will be defeated on the field of its own choice as well as transcendentally. For the divine existence is not only transcendent but immanent, in the world as well as beyond it. The divine consciousness is present here to make this a perfect world and to divinize mankind.

It is the change in consciousness which will accomplish these great and divine intentions. Through this change men and nations will not be then engrossed with their personal or material concerns only. They will not seek only their own development and prosperity, although these are necessary.

They will not seek domination over other men or nations, but both as individuals and as nations will live for the Divine and the world as helpers and leaders for all humanity.

This, Aurobindo says, will bring "the rise of a new, greater, brighter and nobler life for mankind which for its entire realization would rest outwardly on an international unification of the separate existence of the peoples, preserving and securing their national life, but drawing them together in a consummating oneness — finally a new step in the evolution which, by uplifting the consciousness to a higher level, would begin the solution of the many problems of existence which have perplexed and vexed humanity, since man began to think and to dream of individual perfection and a perfect society."[6]

The unification of the human race is in process. Its initiative and its spiritual source are not clearly understood as yet, and the obstacles are vast. It is necessary for some of the very arguments that are advanced against it. Small nations cannot retain their freedom and indeed some of the large nations may be unable to retain their own if a free union of the nations is not achieved. For otherwise and, as human history shows, some totalitarian regime will attempt to conquer the world and rule all under its own banner. It would force upon mankind a disastrous dictatorial hegemony, and enforced autocratic single regime, a monolithic oneness, which would be bound to collapse as all such ruthless empires have in the past. The only way to prevent this is by free international cooperativeness among the nations. Human stupidity and folly might delay but cannot "stand forever against this necessity of nature and the Divine Will."

"Nationalism will then have fulfilled itself — an international spirit and outlook must grow up and international forms and institutions, which today are gradually increasing in number and scope and operate with mutual satisfaction and credit in many fields. The spirit of nationalism can find these things perfectly compatible with the legitimate protection of the freedom of the individual and the nation and the integrity of their outlook — a new spirit of unity will be ushered in for the human race."[7]

This is no idle dream which some pessimistic theologians and some misguided statesmen put off to another world and an after-life. Perfect

[6]A. B. Purani, *The Life of Sri Aurobindo* (Pondicherry: Sri Aurobindo Ashram Press, 1960), pp. 271-272.
[7]Anilbaran Roy, *The Gita,* (Pondicherry: Sri Aurobindo Ashram Press, 1954) p. 95.

spiritual freedom for men, and a perfect and free society are to be won here on earth and enjoyed in human life both individual and communal. "The Kingdom of God," said Christ, "is at hand."

This hope is already held by people of vision throughout the world. The difficulties in its way are tremendous, but no more so than other enormous leaps in the evolutionary past. Was it not a vast, earth-shaking change when life emerged on this planet from the dust of the earth? It may take another earth-shaking event, but the unification of man will transpire also. The obstacles are there to be surmounted, as obstacles have been overcome in previous advances. But if this evolution is to take place, it must come through a change, a growth in consciousness, which alone can bring these results for the future of the world.

How soon this can be done, and whether it will be done by peaceful cooperation instead of violent enforcement in terrible circumstances, is something that men must decide.[8] In the Book of Exodus, God tells Moses that the folly the Hebrews had committed in worshipping the golden calf was such that he should destroy them; but Moses reminded God that he did not bring the Hebrews out of Egyptian bondage for mischief but to fulfill a great covenant, and God forgave them.[9] Similarly, human folly or delusion today will not prevent human unification, for man is not created for mischief but to rise to the good, the Infinite, the Eternal.

It was this higher consciousness in himself to which Christ referred when he said to those who fell away from his teachings: "I am from above; you are from below." "If God were your Father you would love me," he said, "for I proceeded and came forth from God; I came not of my own accord but He sent me — he who is of God hears the words of God — the reason that you do not hear them is because you are not of God."[10]

[8] Anilbaran Roy, *The Gita*, (Pondicherry: Sri Aurobindo Ashram Press, 1954) pp. 273-274.
[9] Exodus 32:10-14.
[10] John 8:42-47.

CHAPTER XVI

EPILOGUE

EPILOGUE

APHORISMS

I

1. **Who,** by thinking, can go further than the limits of the mind? It is like the difference between thinking of a journey to a great city and actually going there. You may have thoughts of God. But the real traveler meets the Divine through the soul that covers the greatest distances and never tires.

2. **Make** your mind quiet, calm and peaceful, silent. Then it can receive from above and give right mental form to ideas. Then it will not be a torrent of disturbances and restlessness and wrong ideas.

3. **Begin** your quest for the Divine by quieting the mind. Nothing can take root in a quaking mind. If the Divine is to out-flower in your life, the mind foundation must be stable.

4. **With** a firm will, make your mind a stillness. Let the content of your mind be an unbroken and invulnerable peace. Then it can act with power in the light and strength it receives from above, and in the intensest activity will not lose its calm.

5. **The** mind was not meant to be your master nor thought your chains. If you have firm faith and unbending resolve you can gain control over the mind and freedom from all restlessness.

6. **To** master your mind, to control its wanderings, to insulate it against outside attacks, four things are necessary: no restlessness or disturbance, a calm unmoved state, a settled harmonious rest and deliverance, a silence and stillness no outer action can shatter or change.[1]

7. **Silence** in the mind is greater than quietness. The silent mind is more than controlled. It keeps thoughts unuttered and afar. Thus room is provided for the silence of God to descend into your mind. From the secret and unutterable spirit within, you then think and express, act and live, with flawless perfection and compassion for all.

II

1. **It** is no slander upon you that your mind was once less than it now is. But it would be failure if your mind did not become more than it now is. That is evolution.

2. **One** can accept the facts of science without rejecting the truths of religion. Religion takes man further than science. But science is one of the great bridges over the deep gorges of ignorance that religion must cross on the journey to the Divine.

3. **If** the world were perfect, we might consider our mind as now constituted to be perfect. But the world is not now perfect; a new life is necessary, and for that a new power in man beyond the mind is necessasry. This is what is meant by over-laying the mind — a super-layer of new consciousness.

4. **Rocks,** plants, animals, man — such is the ascending order around us. The next step upward is the new man. We shall have divine knowledge. where present man is limited to mental knowledge. So shall you be born again,[2] and the world.

---

[1] Sir Aurobindo, *Bases of Yoga* (Pondicherry: Sri Aurobindo Ashram Press, 1955) p. 9.

[2] John 3:3.

140

5. **Tremendous** and wonderful seem the advances, the changes, in the outer world. But they will be small compared with what is to result from the change to the higher knowledge within man. For then his spiritual force will purify as it builds, and unite as it liberates.

III

1. **One** should have no hatred, slander, or persecution against other religions or the harmless adherents of other faiths. Religion is not a form of rivalry or a contest for supremacy.

2. **God** is not compressed in a dogma or confined in a chronicle. Preserve and venerate the holy scripture of the past, but look on them as seeds from which greater harvest is yet to grow.

3. **As** to these aphorisms, read them to exceed them.

4. **Perfect** yourself in mind, emotions, and body. Only when you are perfect without will you manifest the perfect soul within. The immortal within shall be transmitted to your outer being.

5. **Be** joyful, for perfection overcomes melancholy, drives our fear; and listen for the voice of love.

6. **One** who unfolds his spirit should discern that it is revealed to the outer eye and in the life of the world.

7. **One** should not neglect one's own needs nor be indifferent to the needs of others.

8. **Be** not of those who claim that with their own hands they shall build heaven on earth. Nor be of those who believe that heaven is always elsewhere and never destined for an evil earth. Rather be among those whose destiny is to render the earth the perfect habitation of the spirit. They shall bring oneness to the world.

9. **Your** purpose on earth is not ignoble nor limited, and you are not here to flee the task. The labor is great, the wonders of the world vast, and vaster yet shall be the fruits of your labors. For God has summoned you to unfold a new life and a new glory on earth.

10. **For** this, a higher power of the divine force must descend into you as a new consciousness. The new power will not descend for you alone. It will withdraw unless you aspire to it for all. That is the condition of the divinization of man.

11. **Be** not alarmed by wars or disorders that may persist for a time. As you individually struggle for the Light and shall find it, so it is and shall be with the nations, humanity, the world. The day of unity and peace is preparing for earth, and after the darkness, dawn nears.

12. **Set** no seal on this spiritual teaching as the first, last, only, or final. It is not a seal, but the opening of a way for transformation.

13. **The** priest who seeks to draw people by saying that his faith is the only true one, ends up by driving them away.

14. **Two** errors are common with respect to the accepted prophets: One is to deny that such a prophet had divine vision. The other is to declare that such a prophet had the widest vision God is ever to reveal. The prophet comes to prophesy and not to perpetuate. He is a voice in the golden choir of man's spiritual unfoldment.

IV

1. **The** religions teach men commandments from above, to live and worship the one God, to be just, righteous, merciful, to love others, to submit themselves to God.

2. **These** of old are truly divine commandments. Well should they be obeyed.

3. **Yet** the worship of men strays away from the Divine, and their love also. Does there not still remain much that is injustice, unrighteousness and not righteousness, cruelty and not mercy, hate and not love, revolt instead of submission to God?

4. **Therefore,** be transformed. You must change from the human to the divine nature. Then what before was commanded but imperfectly obeyed, will become the substance of your being and perfectly fulfilled.

5. **If** in faith you believe the commandments, believe also you will be transformed. You will then have no need to be commanded to be what you are. The flower of God blossoms in the divine garden, and there is no greater beauty to behold.

V

1 **Some** say that ignorance is sin and others that it is an illusion. It is neither. It is a course through which man threads his way to light and truth.

2. **In** the ignorance man must overcome defects within himself and outer obstacles. Thus he everywhere develops strength of resistance, fidelity, will to go through.

3. **Ignorance** is like the earth through which the seedling must burst into the sunlight. It forces man to grow from its lowliness to the heavens.

4. **There** is one champion that ignorance cannot defeat, and that is sincerity armed with knowledge and made invulnerable by love.

5. A small mistake sometimes seems almost unberable to one who seeks the Divine. But he need not fear. This is something more than an endless trial. "This oppostion has been permitted from of old not merely a test or ordeal."[3] It is "a compulsion on us to seek a greater strength, a more perfect self-knowledge, an intenser purity and force of aspiration, a more powerful descent of the Divine Grace."[4] Such are the gifts of ignorance.

6. **It** is the mission of man to realize the Divine on earth, in the world ignorance. Not even the angels were entrusted with such a task. It is to win the earth victory over all that degrades and brutalizes, enslaves and oppresses, disunites and makes hostile; all that is ugly and sordid, self-ish and ignoble, obscure and stupid, ungenerous and petty; all that is impure and mean, that causes the tear to flow and the face to pale. It is to conquer the last enemy, death.[5] This is not the work of angels, safe and unchanging in their astral planes. It is the heroic work of men amid the perils, beauties, and glories of the earth.

7. **By** this conquest there will be established on earth all that ennobles and is merciful, frees and secures, unites and brings peace; all that is grace-ful and beautiful, unselfish and exalted, clear and illumined, generous and great, pure and lofty, all that causes joy and the glad countenance. Such is the divine task of man on the earth. We will not shirk behind the mask of sin or the mist of dream. Through the divine grace we will inherit an earth of oneness.

8. **Therefore,** do not mortify or pain yourself or think of yourself as an impure sinner or an insubstantial dreamer.

---

[3] Sri Aurobindo, *Bases of Yoga* (Pondicherry: Sri Aurobindo Ashram Press, 1955) p. 68.

[4] Ibid., pp. 268-269.

[5] 1 Corinthians 15:26.

9. **Ignorance** is the raw material from which knowledge is made. It is the night and its darkness that awaits the day and its light when all shall see. It is the call from below to which God tenderly responds from above, giving you His love, strength, light, joy, freedom, and immortality in the divine presence.

VI

1. **Love** of the Divine is the shortest path to deliverance, both for you who start early and you who start late.

2. **He** who chooses the path of love will find that wisdom hastens to help, and action does not tarry to bring him swiftly to the Divine.

3. **He** who has this love recognizes knowledge as his pilot and action as his rudder on the divine voyage. But the passenger is love, the cargo is love, and the haven is love.

4. **Surrender** yourself entirely to the Divine. All that you thus give will be purified, while all that you hold back will become as dross.

5. **To** him who makes the Divine surrender, God makes in return the greater gift of Himself. You give yourself, and God will not let you be more generous than He is.

6. **He** who gives nothing to the Divine, not himself, nor anything that he has or does, falls on many thorns; but he who gives himself and serves God with what he has and does, is called blessed.

7. **If** you lose your way, love of the Divine will lead you safely. If you are engulfed by despair, it will restore your courage. If you doubt, it will rekindle your faith. If you cannot see, it will remove your veil.

8. **To** love humanity is kindness, while to love God is all of this, and heaven on earth.

9. **Love** among all nations is the peace of freedom, while love of God is all of this, and the joy of the immortal.

10. **Love** of the Divine and love of mankind are inseparable.

THE TRANSFORMED

1. **Be** transformed. This goal man has had before him from of old, but has not reached because of the distance to it. But the distance shortens and the hour grows near, even though the last steps of the long journey may seem the most tiring and the hardest. Oneness on earth is bound to come. Transformed men are bound to bring it.

2. **The** transformed man is no longer the pawn of passion, the dupe of ignorance, the slave of the body.

3. **Your** present self has done well for you, but it is not your highest. Receive now a new consciousness, a new power that can guide you far beyond the enclosures of ignorance.

4. **You** are not a prisoner longing for release from the world, and a distant hereafter. You are free to be released even here, perfected on earth, an equal to your soul in the timeless and the eternal.

5. **He** who is transformed is like a factory manager who tears out old and obsolete machinery, and replaces it with new equipment. He tears out cupidity, wrath, and torpor. He rebuilds with unselfishness, calmness, strength. Then all people come to his door and buy his product, and his competitors hasten to find the secret of his success. If you are transformed, re-made, all people will find in you the secret of divine victory.

6. **Give** up stubborn dogma, frenzied heresy, cynical indifference. These are children of the mind and destroyers of human happiness. The transformed individual is guided by the light of the soul, and not the opinions of the mind. He is skillful and unerring. He is like a workman who knows his trade, knows his tools, knows his materials, knows what to do and what not to do, and no one can equal him in his work, which is the work of God.

7. **He** who is transformed loves all but does not accept the errors of any. He hates none but defeats injustice, tyranny and the oppression of any.

8. **He** who is transformed sees that great teacher guide him to the greater teacher within himself, to the soul that stands near to God. The finger of transformation points within and above.

9. **To** transform yourself you must aim also for the transformation of all others. Otherwise the change, both in you and in them, is not possible in the fullest.

10. **He** who is transformed is matchless in serenity, strength, firmness; he is radiant with joy, love, and power from the illimitable, the Divine.

11. **He** who is transformed is like a runner in a relay race who hands his torch to a new and fresh runner. But the new runner is his own new consciousness that never tires or loses, that wins every race and the supreme laurel.

12. **He** who is transformed is like an army whose siege is lifted, a saint whose crown of thorns is lifted, a man whose sorrow is lifted from his heart and ignorance from his brow.

13. **The** transformed man is unvexed by past, present, or future. From the past he learns correction. In the present he charts the course. As to the future, it is the gateway to the immortal.

14. **One** cannot be transformed without the aid of the divine grace and force. To change your nature from the human to the Divine requires the divine touch, the spiritual caress, the Infinite skill.

15. **If** you call for transformation, God brings it to you with His love. If you do not call, He waits patiently until you are ready, until the flame of divine adoration leaps up on the altar of your soul.

16. **Mind,** nerves, body, all must be transformed. A partial transformation leaves disfiguration in the nature.

17. **The** transformed man who perfects himself, who perfects humanity and the earth, fulfills the destiny of his soul. He completes the task God has given him, and embodies the divine truth. Among men they are the highest, the incomparable, the perfected.

By these things is this spirituality realized:

1. Love for the Divine, oneness with God;

2. Love for all beings, oneness with all creatures;

3. Overcoming narrow egoistic demands and actions;

4. Entering into wide consciousness of all existence;

5. Descent of divine light and power to overlay the mind;

6. Transformation and perfection of your nature through descent of the divine force;

7. For these things opening and aspiration to the force is necessary, but all is made possible for you through divine grace. Call from below and the victory will descend to you from above. Whatever the obstacles, aspire and all else will be done for you.

SELF-KNOWLEDGE AND SOCIAL ACTION

By Obadiah Silas Harris

SELF-KNOWLEDGE AND SOCIAL ACTION

By
Obadiah Silas Harris

Change has everyone in a spin. It threatens at any moment to completely overwhelm us. . .

Stop a moment! Catch your breath! From a storehouse of ideas old and new, Eastern and Western, scientific and spiritual, Dr. Obadiah S. Harris has woven a tapestry of the process of change.

This engrossing volume attempts to define and describe the structure of human personality and the meaning and process of its growth in its triune proportions — individually, socially and transcendentally.

This is a book with a genuinely universal appeal. It is addressed to community educators as the "agents of change." But the message that all changes, large and small, must begin with a change in consciousness of one individual has significance for everyone. Every educator, and every sincere person concerned with man's free and harmonious social-cultural development should have this book for serious study.

TABLE OF CONTENTS

ISBN 74-83467
1974 ©

$5.95
111 pp.